Francisco Goya

Pierre Descargues

GOYA

CRESCENT BOOKS
New York

CONTENTS

Illustrations

CHAPTER I

THE SPANIARD

Self-Portrait,
Agen Municipal Museum, 1783

Spanish painting occupies a place in the history of European art but has always been a little apart in its style and development. Art-lovers in 18th century Europe learned about Spanish painting mainly from reproductions in books. Works by Bosch, Titian, Rubens, Tibaldi, Cambiaso and Tiepolo had been imported and the neo-classical style of these pictures had influenced Spanish art, but even so it was regarded as different from other European art. However, in the early 19th century political upheavals in Spain threw great numbers of paintings from Spanish convents and churches on to the art market. Thus three centuries of Spanish painting came into circulation at once. People began to appreciate the Caravaggio-like style of Ribera, the delicate paintings of Murillo, and the austere works of Zurbaran and of El Greco in which the stern faces burn with divine fire.

This enormous quantity of works coming on to the market encouraged the idea that Spain was a strange country beyond the Pyrenees, linked by tradition with the West Indies and Arabia, and that the life-style of the Spanish was closer to that of the Middle East than of Europe. Spain was thus regarded as the most different, perhaps the wildest, country in Europe. It was a European nation whose exotic character could be enjoyed, while an underlying sense of security was given by its deep-rooted Christianity. In other words, people were aware of Spain's differences rather than its similarities to other European countries.

Goya became the most Spanish of the painters of the period. His work is tragic, full of gleaming knives, dark caps concealing faces, fans fluttered in little white hands, guitars, bullfights. The bloody side of religion is there too: the Inquisition was losing ground, and so we do not know whether the chained and whipped bodies are those of saints canonised by the Church or of apostates and heretics. The angels have a sweetness that is more feminine than masculine; the beautiful ladies and their maids are dressed in white and gold as though in a human paradise. Goya can also express horror, and the rituals he shows are not always Christian.

His art could easily illustrate a travel brochure: wine, flamenco, bullfights, a rose in a mantilla, a duel with knives, Don Juan, the Cid a chord on the guitar. It is like a tourist's dream. Goya painted portraits of the greatest *toreros* of his time, drew or engraved the most glorious moments of the bullfight, painted the most beautiful listeners to serenades, dancers of the seguidilla or the fandango, sad kings and gloomy hidalgos. There are legends about his life that could have inspired the poet Lorca or filled a chapter of a picaresque romance: the abduction of girls, the perilous love of duchesses, duels in the streets, pursuits across rooftops, mortal danger in the face of black bulls. Everything we might read in the wild romances of Gil Blas of Santillana has been attributed to him. Toledo blades, Cordova leather, dry wine that catches the breath, drunk from a crystal goblet, black lace with bright drops of blood—Goya has become and remains a tourist attraction. But if poets and chroniclers have invented fantastic events which may have taken place in Goya's youth and the obscure years of his maturity, it

is not without reason. If these adventures have been grafted on to his life, we have to realise that something must have given rise to these legends. His existence must have been romantic to accord with his works. Archives tell us about his official career. The painter's letters tell us of his delight at having kissed the hands of the royal family. How can official documents and letters explain a picture which shows people loving, fighting, ascending to paradise or going down to hell? The Goya legend is simply a biographical commentary on his works.

There is nothing like this to lend colour to the careers of Zurbaran, Le Brun, David or Corot. We cannot deny that Goya's art is intensely Spanish. But we must realize that in many ways he was no different from his contemporaries, Füseli, Blake, David, Gros, Hogarth and Raeburn. For instance, he painted certain war scenes; other scenes from the same war were painted by foreign artists. This is not something exclusive to his period. When Frans Hals was painting the arquebusiers of Haarlem, Velasquez was painting the capitulation of the Dutch forces at Breda. What is there to separate Gros, who in 1810 depicted the surrender of Madrid to Napoleon, from Goya who in 1814 depicted the revolt of the people of Madrid? Both surrender and revolt happened in 1808. The event painted by Goya took place on March 2nd, that painted by Gros on December 4th. In one we

see the delagates from Madrid kissing the ground in front of the Emperor, in the other, the same Spaniards are fighting Mamelukes who seem to have come straight out of a picture by Gericault or Vernet. The resemblances are so striking that we even get the impression that Gros copied his Spaniards from Goya, and Goya learnt his French types from Gros. The faces certainly resemble each other, but perhaps it is enough for an artist to look into his own mind in order to come close to other artists. In those times the artist had to create an image acceptable to his patron of an event at which he was not present. The painting of the period had to be heroic, whether it was produced for Napoleon I or Ferdinand VII. The paintings by Goya and Gros are heroic.

Painting also had to be a record. Art, whether in palaces or in houses, was an adornment, a record, propaganda; a luxury on which many insisted, but which gave no more than could be got from a tailor. In these circumstances art was simply decoration. The art-lover had to feel flattered, because it was mainly his image which was portrayed. It was also the record of his acts and amusements. Certain tapestries by Goya describe worldly scenes in a spirit similar to the pointed irony of Hogarth's ball scenes. In portraits, Goya gives us what appear to be Frederick of Prussia in hunting garb and Madame Adelaide with an enormous hat; they

595.

are really King Charles III and Queen Maria Luisa. There is Madame Recamier on her day-bed and Josephine meditating in the forest, her breast palpitating under the light shawl. There is a vibrant Marquesa of Santa Cruz, with a lute in her hands. Another, like a doll taken out of the box, is the Marquesa of Pontejos. In Goya's work we also find soldiers similar to those painted by Reynolds in Great Britain, Wojniakoski in Poland, Gericault in France. Then there are garden parties: the famous *Field of San Isidro* is not very different from the picnic of the court of Stanislas Augustus on the banks of the Vistula, painted by Belotto, nor from the fashionable open-air parties in which Magnasco kept alive a tradition dear to Velasquez, nor from de Troy's hunting lunches.

We wonder then whether it was because Goya was official painter to the Spanish court, as David was to Napoleon, that his work is comparable to that of his contemporaries? The function may have given rise to similarities. There are affinities between Goya's hunting king and the country gentlemen who posed for Gainsborough. People play on swings in J. B. Huet's tapestries as they walk on stilts in Goya's painting. Is the Goya employed by the royal family the true Goya? Surely not; the true Goya is the engraver of the *Disparates*, the *Caprichos*, *The Disasters of War*, a man in revolt and at the same time a wise man disappointed with the world he lived in. And certainly not the man who painted portraits of the king.

This idea of Goya is very widespread today because we prefer the free man to the king's man. Does not Goya's death away from Spain, perhaps lead to to consider him in this way? He fled from a world in which, though famous, he was still the servant of his betters. He left Spain to follow a path he had set foot upon years before. He needed to abandon the dependent position which made him like other artists employed in other European courts.

Thus Goya moved towards solitude, towards withdrawal from the world and its daily round. Rembrandt too felt the same in the face of the burghers of Amsterdam. Both moved away from different social orders. Very often the artist, wherever he may be, has this need for introspection to find his own path. At this point art serves man's cause all the better through the struggle of the artist towards personal truth. It is well known that we habitually consider the past only as it affects the present; when we see, as we so

Füseli 1741–1825—*View of a hospital, etching
taken from the collection Galerie des Arts et de
l'Histoire of Reveil, Paris 1836*

Delacroix 1799–1863—*Dante and Virgil guided by
Flegias,
Louvre, Paris, 1822*

often do, the young thoughtlessly seeking novelty, we maintain that old age is the moment at which the innovator sees the triumph of his ideas. The traditional notion of the artist's career is based on the concept of initial rejection transformed into later success. Maturity tolerates, though with a sigh, the honours of a society remorseful that it could not at first understand Picasso and Gauguin. Goya completed his work when success had already smiled on him, and so did Rembrandt and Titian.

Later we shall give a more exact picture of Goya as a man of the opposition, a solitary. Even in this more personal part of his work, Goya was not alone. The imaginative side, the communication with the unknown, can be found in Füseli, whose unconscious mind gave birth to monsters, in Blake who painted things beyond reality, in Delacroix who followed Dante and Virgil to hell. Delacroix painted a tiger ripping open the belly of a horse, Gericault painted the severed heads of executed men. Goya was not only of his own time, but went beyond all other artists in exploring the depths of the human mind, where there is freedom for the rebellious spirit. Like Rembrandt, he often painted two different works simultaneously, one commissioned, the other for himself. Obviously he must have put more of himself into one picture than into the other, but he was always present

in both: in the tapestry cartoons for the apartments of the princes of the Asturias, as in that profile of a dog painted on the wall of his own house against a background of yellow sky, which seems to prefigure the plays of Samuel Beckett; in the flashes of light which seem to tear through the black threads of mantillas, and the grey silk of gowns, as in the undulating, shadowy forms of threatening crowds. There are many sides to Goya; we may prefer one to another, but none of them can be ignored.

CHAPTER II

PRECURSORS AND FOLLOWERS

Goya's life fell between two centuries—he lived from 1746 to 1828—and he is considered more Romantic than Voltairian, more of the 19th than the 18th century. He was the first artist of a new world; he was born ten years before and died a year after Beethoven. When young Goya had his first disappointment in the examination for admission to the San Fernando Academy in Madrid (he was seventeen), Tiepolo had been invited to Madrid and was working there. Thus there were two artists in the same city at the same time, one belonging to a new world and the other to a world which was soon to be forgotten. Between them was the master chosen by the royal palace and made responsible for all the art in the kingdom, Raphael Mengs, a neo-classical artist, but one endowed with great good sense. He is said to have been the link between Goya and Tiepolo. A genius about to be outdated and another genius in embryo co-exist uneasily. For historians there is no boring art. All painting is the subject of eager study, and so in Madrid in 1764 we find, not very far distant one from the other, the heir of Veronese and the precursor of Manet.

Through these artists two centuries and two worlds are linked, different both in their sensibility and in the forms in which they are expressed. But they are very close to each other, since Tiepolo engraved Caprichos, and Goya painted church ceilings; the Italian appeared to seek for fantastic subjects, while the Spaniard painted priests sacrificing to Vesta.

Tiepolo subsequently turned from the baroque to neo-classicism with great spectacular subjects, and Goya began to paint strange pictures of witches flying over rivers, showers of bulls, beggars in meditation, and other fantastic types of humanity. Both ignored the rules and transcended any kind of formula, and in this they are profoundly linked despite their many differences.

Who are Goya's precursors? The historian's opinion may depend on his nationality; if he is Italian he will insist on Tiepolo and those who followed him. He will also speak of Magnasco because of the fantastic element, Fra Galgario who painted with his fingers, Alessandro Longhi the portraitist, or Rosalba Carriera. If the author is French, he will remember that in Spain the court painters were French: Michelangelo Houasse, Jean Ranc, Louis Michel van Loo, little known even in France. Between Philip IV's family by Velasquez and Charles IV's family by Goya, comes Philip V's family by van Loo. Houasse, a true chronicler of the Spanish landscape, may have influenced Goya's landscapes. Another Frenchman, Parrocel, can be considered a precursor of Goya in his pictures of violent subjects. The English see the influence of Blake, Gainborough and Lawrence. But French art was disrupted by the Napoleonic Wars, and the Italians have no very famous painters in the 19th century. In other words, there are precursors without many similarities. The difficulty consists in finding a common origin and a relationship without the intrusion of too many differences.

Until the end of the 19th century, the Paris salon catalogues always gave the precursors of those exhibiting. The name of the master was indicated for each artist. Corot was considered a pupil of Bertin, Rembrandt a pupil of Lastman, Velasquez of Pacheco, and van Dyck of Rubens. Goya was a pupil of Luzan and Bayeu. From them he learnt the art of painting—how to turn out rapid work on different subjects, and the easiest ways to satisfy the customers' demands. Then came a higher ambition—to enter the King's service. There was, however, no question of exclusive patrons—either the Church or the King—as we shall see later. It has often been the case that the success of the pupil offends the master, and as the master seeks to outshine his pupils, the pupil takes pleasure in the master being forgotten.

Besides Luis Menendez, known for his portraits and still life, and Luis Paret, chronicler of court life, there are many Spanish artists contemporary with Goya: Camaron, Gomez Esteve, Lopez Maella, Carnicera. But none of their works is of very great importance. Sometimes we see Tiepolo's influence; sometimes a little romanticism, eyes full of tears, affected gestures, sometimes a deceptive conformism in portraits, that is to say the influence of other artists, but without originality. In short, there is uncertainty about Goya's precursors, and contemporary Spanish artists were undistinguished.

L. Paret 1746–1799—*The Luncheon of Charles III,*
undated,
Prado, Madrid

However, isolated though he was in his own time, we shall see Goya's artistic stature increasing as he succeeded in achieving truth in expression. Goya belonged to his period, a period in which classical forms were dissolving, losing their structural power, and painting no longer had any organic unity. It was a period of crisis in form; intellectual crises were constantly imminent. The ferment of the 18th century was to lead to the birth of a new policy, a different ethic, a different society; it gave rise also to a change in aesthetic forms. If we look, for example, at a picture by De Troy or Lancret or Guardi or a royal luncheon depicted by Luis Paret, we see an artificial world. As Starobinski writes: "before the painter takes up his brushes, how many artists have already had a hand in the scene, from the architect to the wigmaker, from the jeweller to the shoemaker". The wealthy lived surrounded by decoration of every style, which was used to create a delightful world of fantasy into which they could escape. Chinese art was very popular and co-existed alongside illustrations of Ancient Greek and Roman themes. And of course there was also much religious art inspired by Christian traditions. However, the interest in antiquity predominated. People began to find ruins picturesque and romantic. Painters thus learned to include Roman columns and Greek urns in their pictures, and erotic nudes were painted thinly disguised as characters from mythology. A sleeping man with a woman gazing at him was Eros discovered by Psyche. An artist painting a nude was Apelles and Campaspe. Women bathing in a river were Diana and her companions. Anyway, what every man was thinking of was not the goddess, but the titillation of his own desires. These pictures were decorative but had little meaning, and serious problems were evaded. Everything was reduced to pretty shapes and charming colours. Everything was calm, or at least the dramas of the moment were resolved by a purely aesthetic crisis.

There was no menace in either God or the devil. There were wars and famines, but no one would admit it. Thus the leisured classes came to be hated by those less fortunate. The glory of the 18th century forged the weapons that destroyed it.

This world where time was frittered in amusements, where original impulses were unwelcome unless prettily adorned, gave birth to more pictures than frescoes, more statuettes than monuments. They had, alas, forgotten the solemn, splendid art that had lasted for centuries. In this period works of art were almost all lightweight. The characteristics sought by their creators were unknown to the great artists of the preceding period. There had to be an intimate conversation with the spectator. A subject full of light could be seen in all its enchantment, as in Chardin. The movement of the brush-strokes, like a dance, could give life to the picture and express a gesture by a mere hint, as in Fragonard. Light could creep into the colours and make them sparkle, as in Guardi. And in Watteau we can see interruptions in the rhythm, slight breaks separating objects which seen from a distance appear closely united. It was a novelty; but these subtleties, these collusions, these complicities, the various characteristics of the artist who was more concerned with showing off his talents than with the themes he was treating, were a sign of the great disorder of the period. There were still traditional artists applying the old rules and remaining faithful to a great declamatory art. But baroque had made art a synonym of virtuosity, with its perfection, and everyone aspired to novelty. When Goya was born, a new movement in art was attracting attention, proposing fixed, definite rules, with prototypes which could be trusted, and which had been ignored in previous years. Neo-classicism was very successful, and spread all over Europe; the paintings were well-proportioned, balanced in composition, and very colourless. According to Raphael Mengs and his pupils—who sought to achieve order in the field of aesthetics—design must predominate over colour. Colour became a mere superficial covering in which the brush of the virtuoso created shining silks and laces so realistic that the eye was deceived. Works thus created had to have a fine rhythm and great seriousness. There were also dull pictures, made soporific by the application of these principles. Thus began

a period—lasting more than a century—in which every country in Europe revered Grecian art. Every school always comes to a lamentable end; neo-classicism had not even any geniuses.

But this lack did not reduce its effectiveness. In fact the more that certain ideas are upheld by mediocrities, the more open the road seems to be. We can see, for example, the influence of neo-classicism on Tiepolo's elder son, Giandomenico. Giandomenico, who inherited freedom of invention and an equally desirable talent as a colourist, was assailed by strong doubts, and painted frescoes that were almost monochrome, simply because he sought to discipline himself. Another example was Canova, a Venetian who abandoned painting to devote himself to sculpture which was considered to be a purer art by Winckelmann, the movement's theoretician. However, in the last quarter of the century these theories began to lose their influence and there were deviations. For instance, when David went to Rome he worked with Mengs, but also wanted to study drawing with Piranesi. Neo-classicism did not follow one single path: David pointed out another, no less classical, but more vigorous. When the *Oath of the Horatii* appeared in Rome it was said: "At last, a real picture. Until now we have seen only little pictures pleasing to the eye but without either spirit or reason." This picture thus represented a breakthrough. The literature of the time was reflecting modern ideas and events, but art had stagnated. Now it was about to be revitalized.

Flaxman 1755–1826—*The Fury of Athamas,*
Ickworth, Suffolk

Benigno Gagnereaux 1756–1795—*Psyche abducted*
in the Palace of Love,
Dijon Museum

The Prado has many portraits by Raphael Mengs of people with black eyes, fixed and motionless, with clothes carefully pressed for the occasion. Is this characteristic also common to such of Goya's early works as have come down to us? Not at all. Goya's first works are tormented, with a whirling rhythm, in vivid colours, exactly opposite to what the master advised. In 1761 Mengs called F. Bayeu to Madrid. And twelve years later it was Bayeu who summoned Goya, whose works were moving towards calm, well-ordered compositions, but without applying "fixed and definite rules". It will be seen that in his portraits Goya took care not to shock by inviting comparison with those of Mengs. In his compositions Goya seemed to have lost the liveliness of his first church decorations, but he was far from satisfying the laws dictated by the painter of Parnassus.

At this point we must return to the theme of Spain: this country must be considered by the standards of other nations which were open to influences from abroad. Charles III and Charles IV had played a part in Spain similar to that of the Sovereigns of Prussia, Poland or Russia—Frederick, Stanislas Augustus, Catherine II. They enticed the most famous artists from all

David 1748–1825—*The Oath of the Horatii,
Louvre, Paris, 1784*

*Sacrifice to Vesta
Gudiol Collection, Barcelona, 1771*

over the world to come and paint at their courts. These artists, who were highly paid for coming, must have suffered considerable disorientation, since although they put their talent in its most authentic form at the disposal of their patrons, they kept some national virtues, which came out fresh and unspoiled. They did not develop their own aesthetic attitude in the country which gave them a home, but stimulated local artists to find strength in their own popular traditions. It was no accident that Lorenzo Tiepolo, the Italian painter's young son, produced pastels of Madrid life, *majos* and orange sellers. It was no accident that Mengs, when in charge of the tapestry workshop, forbade not only the copies of Teniers introduced by a Flemish department head, but also all mythological, Biblical and allegorical subjects. Mengs wanted the cartoons to represent contemporary Spanish life. This was of course only in tapestry, a less noble art than painting, but the fascination of local colour must have been powerful to induce Mengs to give up the fundamental idea that an artist's education should be based on the study of antiquity. Scenes of Spanish popular life were preferred to the motifs of Raphael and the decorations of Pompeii.

The influences on Goya's early style can easily be traced if we do not connect them with the presence of foreign artists in Madrid, and limit ourselves to considering what the artist may have experienced directly in Spain. We must also consider the circumstances under which he received his first commission for tapestry design. He was then aged 30. He had to take into account the work of F. Bayeu, who was 12 years older than he was, and of R. Bayeu, José del Castillo, Barbaza, G. Aguirre, J. de Sales, Agrurra, Nani and Zacaria Gonzalez Velasquez, all of whom were employed by Mengs to provide inspiration for the Tapestry Factory, and who had been working there for more than thirteen years when Goya had his first order. Goya had to adapt himself to a style already well defined and in existence for some time.

Since the 19th century, the destiny of art has largely been decided in capital cities: in the 18th century the life of painting and sculpture was already centred there, but provincial schools were very powerful. Aesthetic conflicts were made known in a less lively, less peremptory way. The interest was in men rather than in their ideas, and strong personalities could develop freely; they could be sure that there would be little change in the general taste for slow progress rather than sudden change. The atmosphere was ideal for a cruising speed rather than for lightning dashes. Accustomed to this stability, Goya, who lived in Saragossa until the

age of 27, never experienced the disorder of 18th century France, and was influenced by his Spanish predecessors. If we find echoes of Tiepolo and affinities with Bayeu in some of the details in his frescoes and tapestries, it is due to compromise rather than to any real purpose. Goya could toy with various styles and trends with a skill which—if we consider what is happening in present-day art, which is more accessible to us—we may venture to call completely Spanish. He never went to any extremes, nor did he follow the broad paths laid down by artists all over the world. It is surprising in a young artist, since usually total dedication to an aesthetic theory is a characteristic of youth. With maturity, the artist usually deserts principles to devote himself to personal realities. He passes, that is, from the general to the particular, having discovered that his microcosm contains the macrocosm. We have to admit that Goya began by shifting for himself.

Was Goya then nobody's son and nobody's brother? Not at all. He was the child of his circumstances and his environment, in Saragossa first of all, and in Madrid later on. Honest parents these, fulfilling well their task of putting a young man into the art world. His affinities are still mysterious. But how is it that his pictures of rebels have something in common with the soldiers of Gros, his marchionesses seem ready for a conversation with those of Reynolds, while they have no point of contact with the characters depicted by his Spanish contemporaries? Because his type of imaginative work accords with that of the English artists, while in his own country it appears to be a rare flower.

Goya, born in 1746, was 20 years younger than Mengs, 17 years younger than Reynolds, 10 years younger than Fragonard, 11 years younger than Greuze, 5 years younger than Füseli, 13 years younger than Hubert Robert, 11 years older than Blake, 10 years older than Rowlandson and 25 years older than Gros. With only two years between them, he was of the same generation as David (1748). And he too, like David, was born into a tradition, at a moment when the pictorial vein was less vigorous; and this sluggishness led posthumously to infinite strength. There are similarities between the careers of David and Goya; both were famous, both were employed at their country's court, and both were obliged to retire abroad, where they died.

Goya's fame came late, at about fifty, like an epilogue to what he had done in thirty years of painting. David first made his name at 36. Today 36 may seem late, but in those times it was not. Let us not forget that these two artists appeared at a moment of separation between two worlds, and without any doubt it was more difficult for them to find themselves as artists at this point in history than at any other time. Neoclassicism appeared like a revolt. David embraced it, and went beyond. Goya followed the genres which he thought it expedient to accept. David evolved rapidly, Goya much more slowly.

This was also because the break occurred in Spain much later than in France, and the two artists worked in different circumstances. Goya was 30 when he delivered the first tapestry cartoon; that is to say when he entered the service of the court. David was 56 when he became the Emperor's first official painter and was given the task of recording ceremonies pictorially, designing costumes and furniture, and working on the decoration of the rooms in the Imperial apartments. Goya had precise orders from the beginning; David did personal research, made possible by the Prix de Rome. The Spaniard, caught in the toils of the court, could give rein to his own personality only after a slow evolution which led him to solitude. For the Frenchman, fame came more rapidly. The Imperial service, in his mature years, gave him a sense of direction. The sudden loss of his employment left the artist without work, incapable of taking up again the values and themes which had contributed to his reputation under the previous regimes.

It could be said that there are situations which one can leave, but from which one does not like to be dismissed.

Goya wished to become an official painter, and he succeeded. Later he ceased to be one. But he remained one for a long time, and in a difficult period in which dynasties were unstable and sovereigns changed frequently. Official portraits had to be swiftly improvised. It is not known whether, in this period of exclusions, resignations and proscriptions, it was age or disgust that caused him to leave his post.

David had glorious followers: Gros, Ingres, Gerard, David d'Angeres, Girodet and Isabey were his pupils. Goya had assistants and disciples. Of those who worked with Goya, no names have survived. And after Goya the line of descent is a strange one.

Eugenio Lucas followed Goya's dark style in scenes of brigandage, carnival, bullfights and witches' sabbaths, and the imitation is so close that many works of Lucas are thought of as being by Goya. This happens also with some pictures by Antonio Elbo and Leonardo Alenzo. This was the prevailing trend, even though Goya had not had much success with it in his lifetime. The picture *The Burial of the Sardine* turns up in a sale in 1808, and is described as a "cabinet painting", that is to say a work of little moment, to be kept in a collection with other works, probably including some by Teniers.

Manet, who was born eight years after Eugenio Lucas, certainly did not see the eight Goyas which comprised the Musée Espagnol. This museum was dismantled in 1848 under King Louis Philippe. Manet said he was very impressed with the paintings of Velasquez, but Goya influenced him, especially in scenes of bull-fighting and the dance, and in portraits of women, all themes peculiar to Goya.

Thirty years after Goya's death, Baudelaire published a study of some foreign caricaturists, and praised Goya as an engraver. Among what he called caricaturists Baudelaire also included Daumier, Hogarth and Bruegel. Goya appeared as an expounder of dreams, an artist who could make the monstrous appear plausible.

Twenty years earlier, seeing Algeciras in the distance, where he could not disembark, Delacroix felt his heart throbbing at the thought of Goya's art. The drawings he made of the *Caprichos* have recently been discovered.

Subsequently the French painters Pharamond Blanchard and Dehodencq developed their romantic vision in Spain by painting the processions of penitents and the festivals of Bodes Reales, thus keeping alive the memory of Goya's *fiestas*, though giving the scenes a more picturesque and worldly character.

Goya's followers can be divided into two groups. One group laid emphasis on the folklore side, and ended, both in music and in painting by falling to a merely tourist level, despite the impact of the *Goyescas* of Granados. The others preferred the fantastic side of Goya's work. The echoes of this second trend kept their power and their purity for a long time, confirming the view that there are some fundamental ideas which disappear, while others remain always pure and uncontaminated.

Lucas 1824–1870—*Inquisition scene,*
Louvre, Paris

E. Manet 1832–1883—*The Spanish Singer,*
Metropolitan Museum of Art, New York

In addition to these widely separated trends, there were also quieter, more considered views of the artist's work which sought to avoid dividing and fragmenting it. Thus in 1842 T. Gauthier published a very objective article in the review, *Cabinet de l'Amateur.* Let us remember that the poet did not usually approach Spanish subjects with much goodwill; for instance when commenting on Manet's *Guitarrero* he began his article with "*Caramba!*" To return to Goya, Gauthier wrote that the artist—the most Spanish of the Spaniards—was a combination of Velasquez and Reynolds. A little earlier, the critic Louis Vierdot, unlike Baudelaire who admired Goya even in caricature, deplored the burlesque aspect of Goya's art, but despite this lack of understanding he placed the artist between Hogarth and Rembrandt, which is indeed his proper place.

This historic evaluation of Goya does not take into account another deciding factor; a deep sympathy and communication had established itself between the artist and his public. This happened through subjects not naturally connected with each other: attacks on stage coaches, murders of women by brigands, madhouse scenes, bullfights, festivals—especially carnivals, witches' sabbaths and the story on six connected panels of the capture of a bandit by a priest, a kind of strip cartoon.

These are themes already treated by others: Botticelli drew Satan and the 15th century artists made woodcuts of the birth of Antichrist. Bosch painted the Beast, and Ingres, encouraged by Leonardo's example, painted a dragon. The capitals of Vezelay show the basilisk, an animal born from a cock's egg fertilised by a toad. Witchcraft is no novelty. Callot depicts brigands, and Longhi carnivals and masked balls, and in popular art there are many pictures showing appalling crimes.

We find murders in Poussin. Gericault was fascinated by the faces of madmen, which he painted with an almost clinical eye. But no one seems to have ventured into the field which we find today in items in the newspapers under the heading "news in brief". These collect together the actions, apprehensions and hopes that spring from the depths of the human mind, and deal with pleasure, death, madness and fear in a form accessible to all. A man who decorated roundabouts for country fairs once told me that his customers usually ordered two series of motifs: erotic and fantastic. In the first case he painted swelling breasts and bare legs, in the second, spectres and fabulous beasts. In Goya we find the same very subtle juxtaposition of eroticism and mystery, the same presentation of the basics of life, the same interest in crime, heroics, madness and masks.

We have seen that executions or masquerades were often depicted in paintings. The Dutch painters of the 17th century frequently illustrated such themes, and so did the Flemish artists of the same period, but always as chroniclers. Goya got his information from news-sheets, from events reported to him, and from what he saw himself. But he did not use them as pretexts for moral instruction. His visits to lunatic asylums had nothing in common with imperial visits to plague victims or with good works and acts of mercy. His ecclesiastical courts are never seen from the point of view of the judge who condemns the guilty to death, but from that of the accused himself. Goya does not approach these themes from the angle of the "right-thinking" man, who has never killed nor blasphemed, and believes that the sun moves round the earth (or vice versa, according to the period). Goya paints Spanish life from the point of view of the sinners, either in politics or religion. He paints the madhouse as though he himself were mad; the fire at the hospital as though he himself had fled from the flames; the execution as though he had been in the firing line.

We have a similar impression of immediacy when we compare his war paintings with those of Napoleon's artists. For the latter, a battle was the operation of an admirably constructed machine; they showed it as the accomplishment of a skilled strategy, a masterpiece of military art. Hence the abstract character of their compositions, the quest for beauty being in the deployment of the columns and the combination of squadrons. For Goya, war is massacre, bloodshed, howls, corpses, the reality of fighting. A rapid examination of art under the Empire may convince us that the picture of war is abstract in the case of victory, becoming realistic at the moment of defeat (see the agonies of Boisdenier). In Goya this stage can come before the battle has even begun. We could call it a pre-romantic stage. Goya wished to give the most total view possible of an event, when he painted kings, queens, ministers, nobles. He was not on the side of royalists or the custodians of law and order. He was dealing with human beings who were in power for the moment; with a hereditary system which could put at the head of a country a capable leader or a nonentity, a great statesman or a nymphomaniac. His position was that of a historian who follows the judgment of the majority, a majority which, apart from any consideration of reverence for the leader, and economic and political motives, does not forget that the prince is a man, with limits and potentialities. Goya is, in fact, very near to that mass mentality of which little is known owing to the difficulty of defining it, and which critics tend not to tolerate in the artist, but in contrast to intellectual, informed thought, it preserves basic ideas and beliefs in their pure state. There are elements in the mass consciousness from which more subtle intellects can deduce elaborate theories. Goya always went back to the foundations of human thought, to the primordial obsessions. Was he not perhaps one of the first artists to show us the crowd, that shapeless, undulating mass capable of any sort of demonstration, an inexhaustible reserve of dynamism?

The representation of the crowd is an element that reveals the position of the artist in society, all through the history of art. The first thing we find in Western art is celestial hosts. We see the opposition between order and disorder in the Last Judgments in which the damned are separated from the elect. The elect are organised in well-disciplined armies; the damned are in lawless, turbulent hordes. Suddenly the ground slips away beneath their feet, and that is the fall.

Smugglers in a Cave
Marquis de la Romana Collection,
Madrid, 1724–1795

The same division applies to earthly events; the conquerors pursuing the enemy forces march in good order. The conquered are in confusion and their squadrons are scattering. We see this even in the *Stele of the Vultures* (Ur, third millennium B.C.) in which the prisoners are a shapeless mass crammed into a small space, as in the *Fall of the Angels* by Le Brun. A picture like Rembrandt's *Night Watch* is a rare example of harmony in disorder. It has been compared to a torrent which has broken its banks and is overflowing into a public square. It is an example of social balance, of deliberate discipline, of unity achieved from heterogeneous elements. Carpaccio (16th century) shows the crowd filing and unwinding all through St Mark's Square in Venice, one behind the other, each with his own individuality. Guardi (18th century) shows us that something has changed; the crowd is no longer a succession of known characters, but a shapeless mass which the Doge's guards are dividing to let their lord pass. Goya too brings into prominence this new phenomenon, the masses. He treats it as something real, not seeking out any internal dynamic structures, but simply bringing out its tumultuous power and following its contours. Examples are the singing procession that makes its way to the Feast of St. Isidore in Madrid, and the nocturnal meeting round the great he-goat. Carnival crowds, crowds fascinated by the pomp of the Inquisition's tribunals, or by the rituals of the bullfight, thoughtless crowds which suddenly spring to life and stab the French horsemen—all this appears in Goya's work with a great depth of feeling; the crowd is like a force which may destroy those who believe themselves to be its masters.

This had never before been expressed with the same intensity. No one had ever considered formlessness as a specific theme standing on its own and not as the starting point for the development of harmony. The crowd fascinated Goya, as did all unpredictable forces, like the bull in the arena or the powers of darkness.

One part of his work shows him concerned with things transcending reason, and beyond perception itself. Goya was a good Christian, but not a lover of the clergy, and we may suppose that like all Spanish liberals he judged them severely.

But Goya was very skilled in producing what was expected of him, and what would be useful in his official career. However, when he was a free-lance, he no longer bothered to compose his pictures according to any formal rules. It is not that he was no longer capable of it, having learned this method in his youth and having proved his mastery innumerable times as a Court and Church painter. It was simply that he now wanted to paint an image that was powerful in itself, even though the intensity was often achieved at the expense of clarity.

In this he freed himself from the dictates of his predecessors, especially Tiepolo, and overthrew academic principles. He was probably the first to oppose the academicism which, since Raphael, had united artists in a long uninterrupted chain. Goya broke the continuity with a completely modern idea, the presumption of which Valery condemned. Valery wrote: "To construct a poem containing only poetry is impossible. If a work contains only poetry it is not constructed; that is to say it is not a poem."
I do not mean by this that Goya tried to paint a picture that was just a display of painting technique and nothing else, but he freed himself from many elements which he considered superfluous, whereas before him they were considered indispensable to the artist if he wished to be understood. When his work became known—and not only the engravings which soon spread throughout Europe—the effect of the rough, direct images, breaking away in both subject and composition from rules based on classical art, was to hasten the end of all the contrivances which artists had used to obtain their pictorial expression.

Goya always worked in his own period and never painted anything either classical or Oriental. He did not paint people dressed as Turks or Greeks. His exoticism stopped at Indians killing a Canadian missionary; but these naked savages were not very different from his lunatics gesticulating in madhouses. Whether he showed military men in general's uniform, ladies in gowns made by great dressmakers, or poor devils bereft of reason, he always showed people of his own time, as a deliberate attempt to cast away tradition and break with classical mythology.

Was classical tradition powerful enough in Spain to cover every event with a veil of mythology? This is not the place to discuss that: but we may remark that despite the presence of many Italian artists and Italian works, Spain, through her own artists, rejected the mythological disguise, the detachment from real life, in which foreign artists had become expert. There are shepherds in Velasquez, but they live in Spain and not in Arcady.

Goya threw wide a door that was already

open: the Majas on the balcony are no more than
a sequel to Murillo's *Young Girl and Governess*
at the window. Life continued to be represented
without academic complications, but the relationship between the event and the picture was
more direct, more vivid, whether the subject
was this world or the next, plain to the eye or
hidden. Tradition never recovered from this
influx of reality. It was this immense truth, this
everyday legend, this real life, that Delacroix
and Manet were to appreciate most of all in
Goya's Spain.

Spain had given to art the solemn mysticism
of Zurbaran and the metaphysical impressive-
ness of El Greco. Goya was very interested in
folklore considered as pure truth and introduced
into art the truth about Spain, in all its crudity.
Festivals in town and country formed a procession which was to meet with the Doge's
festivals in Venice and the festivals in France
around the tree of Liberty. These three different
types of dance and song could never have mixed.
Popular truths are more difficult to export than
aesthetic truths.

The truth in Goya's pictures had one great
strength besides its value as evidence. It showed
the great crimson flames of primordial terror
and violence. It brought to painting, at last, a
primitive power and realism that was to dra-
matically change the future of art.

Chapter III

THE EVOLUTION OF A GENIUS

The house at Fuendetodos has a stone tablet outside it with the inscription: Here Francisco was born, 30/3/1746. We are in Aragon, a few miles from Saragossa. There is church and a few houses. Around them is a parched land with dead trees and only a few small herds. Further off there are the ruins of a Moorish castle. It is one of those places which makes a traveller wonder how anyone could ever have come to live there. Its poverty is surprising, since a few minutes' drive away, along the banks of the Ebro, there are fertile, well cultivated fields. Here life is gloomy, destined for hopelessness. There must be serious reasons for living there: despair of life or one's fellow-men, or perhaps it was once a garrison, guarding a pass.

On the naked hills the intense heat of summer brings stones to the surface, while in winter rocks crack with the frost. In the village there is water, which means that life is possible in a region crushed by the seasons. Looking at that house, that remote village on its wretched hill, we think of Goya, forty years later, leaving for the Royal Palace of Madrid with a four-wheeled gig drawn by two mules. His social ascent seems all the greater when we think of the very poor conditions of his birthplace. But Goya was not born in such very great poverty, and he did not attain to fabulous riches.

Not much is known of his family, whose genealogical tree is as dry as the deserts of Aragon. His mother's family, the Lucientes, of Aragonese stock, were *hidalgos*, a social class that was proud but unproductive and not always well off. On his father's side, Basques who had moved to Aragon, there is no trace of nobility.

José Goya, the artist's father, was born in 1713 and was a gilder at Saragossa. In 1735 he married Gracia Lucientes who gave him six children: Rita, Tomas, Jacinto, Mariano and Camilo. They were all born at Saragossa except Francisco. The reason for this different birthplace is unclear, but one possible explanation is that the family had to flee into the countryside after reverses in business; the gilder had to become a farmer. But farming what? Rye perhaps; or perhaps he bred sheep. Another theory is that he became a seller of ice and water. It has also been thought that he came to the mountains for his health.

There is something inexplicable about this birth in a remote village where it could not have been advisable to take a pregnant woman. And the historian may wonder whether the gilder gilded pictures, altars or furniture. The first ceiling to be gilded, with the first gold to be imported from America, was done at Saragossa. There was a tradition in this noble trade which was very near to painting. The elder Goya could have worked on the decoration of Our Lady of the Pillar at Saragossa while his son painted the small cupolas of the principal nave. But the work of this gilder, despite the historians, remains unknown.

As for the family's social position, it is known that Francisco was a pupil at a religious school, the Escuelas Pias, also attended by his brothers. One of them became a priest. The trade of gilder could not have been such a lowly one if one of the sons, Tomas, wished to learn it from his father. We can conclude, then, that the Goya family was middle class and lived on the income from the father's work and the revenue from a family estate. We cannot therefore think of young Goya as a peasant boy leading sheep to pasture or looking after pigs. The painter had a strong constitution, broad shoulders, fists of iron and a thick head of hair. This is known not so much from the self-portraits, because although portraits tell us a great deal, they give us no idea of the model's size. It has been known since the opening of his tomb at Bordeaux where his skeleton showed that he had the build of a giant.

This giant was certainly not one of those Aragonese types whose heads, according to tradition, are so hard that they could be used for hammering in nails. The Marquis of Espinar would not have been glad to have had a brute for a grandfather, and he often boasted of being Goya's descendant.

Thus in three generations the house of Goya, having left Fuendetodos, had risen to a palace with a coat of arms over the door, and a correspondingly high standard of living. But the painter stopped halfway. His letters are full of emotion every time the king is friendly towards him, or a minister stops his carriage to speak to him, or he reaches another stage in his glorious career: member of the Academy, assistant director of painting at the Academy, and then in 1799 first painter of the Royal Bedchamber—this was his highest rank. He went no further, and never became director general of the Academy because of the changing currents of favour and disfavour which formed in government circles.

But what security he had: governments totter,

Velasquez 1599–1660—*View of Saragossa,*
Prado, Madrid, 1647

but the first painter of the Royal Bedchamber seems immovable. Kings change: Charles III, Charles IV, Joseph, Ferdinand VII. The painter remained until four years before his death when he realised that he could not go on, and asked permission to leave the court where he had been employed for thirty years. The dignity of the rank had declined; for the last ten years it had not meant much, and was only a title from the King, as from one gentleman to another. With great courtesy he played his part to the last, and asked for his release for reasons of health. It was granted to him, together with a pension.

But how did Goya become a painter? Unlike today, to be an artist in 18th century Spain was to be part of an established profession. It was therefore quite usual for a boy to think of becoming an artist. Such a profession guaranteed a solid education and an acceptable social position. At that time it was natural to begin a trade at an early age. Goya was twelve or thirteen when he entered the workshop of José Luzan, an artist in Saragossa, to learn to paint. He stayed there for four years, during which he learned all the basic techniques of painting: how to grind the colours, stretch the canvas, and put in the background. He certainly learned an excellent technique, if we think of the state of preservation of his pictures. Luzan, a painter at the time of the Inquisition, was not a man to invite trouble. He respected the wishes of monks who disapproved of some of his nudes, and so he painted light veils over them. It was a stupid business, the effect of which was to ensure that there were few nudes in Spanish painting. However, this concealment was so skilfully done that later restorers were able to remove the chaste retouches. Goya acquired a perfect technique in this school, especially in oil painting.

We do not know what Goya's first attempt at painting was; he had certainly noticed what a variety of subjects his master had to treat: portraits, church decoration, altarpieces, the decoration of drawing-rooms. Painting was fashionable in Saragossa, and everything possible was adorned with it. Painters had as much work as smiths, gilders and carpenters. Goya was never to forget the obvious ubiquity of art in everyday life. Luzan had taught him to carry out the most varied orders. This indicated that Spanish artists had confidence in the range of their abilities, a confidence which was not common to the artists of other countries—for instance, the Dutch were predominantly portraitists. Unlike Rembrandt, who found the subjects for his pictures by dressing up his own friends and relatives or by looking into a mirror —that is, limiting himself to an intimate type of work—Goya, when he began to paint, knew he would have to deal with different forms of artistic expression. That does not mean that he accepted them all.

In 1868 Zapater and Gomez published the *Noticias biograficas* which records interviews with people who remembered Goya. It does not, however, record some of the wilder escapades attributed to him, particularly a flight with a nun to Madrid, but it does record that

the young artist had done a painting in the Reliquary Chapel at Fuendetodos. This showed hosts of angels and clouds with celestial radiance shining from them. In the background is St. Vincent de Paul, the Virgin of Carmel, and the apparition of the Virgin in the vision which St. James had in Saragossa on 2nd January in the year 40. This painting by the young Goya was destroyed in 1936. Photographs show the remarkable skill he possessed, considering that he must have been aged between 15 and 17. At that time he was more interested in the subject than in the technique, in the idea rather than in the precise method of carrying it out.

Luzan was not Goya's only teacher; there was also Saragossa, a great and beautiful city. The first beautiful things to strike the young painter were probably the baroque doorway of the church of his school, and the altars before which he was taught to kneel, and which are still there. During his childhood he saw the enlargement of the Church of Our Lady of the Pillar, which he was later to decorate. In the cathedral were examples of Romanesque, Gothic and Renaissance art, and in the city many towers showing Moorish influence. Oriental art appeared in one of the oldest palaces built by the Arabs in Spain, the Aljaferias (11th century) with a garden surrounded by 17 towers. The Aljaferias had been given these luxurious finishing touches by the Catholic kings. In Goya's time it was used as a barracks, though its Moslem decorations remained intact. We must assume that Goya was influenced—perhaps unconsciously—by Oriental art.

He followed the example of Francisco Bayeu, a Saragossa painter twelve years older than himself, who had left for Madrid to compete several times for a scholarship to study at the Academy, and was on the point of succeeding: he entered the Academy in 1765. Bayeu thus showed Goya what he must do to avoid being stuck in Saragossa, where Luzan had unfortunately remained. Madrid was a place where he could find better conditions for both painting and living.

In 1763, at the age of 17, Goya left for Madrid and entered the competition for the Academy of San Fernando. If Saragossa had had its own Academy he would probably have stayed there, but Saragossa did not open its Academy until 1792.

The Madrid Academy was founded in 1751, and brought together Spanish painters, sculptors and architects; lessons were given, scholarships were awarded, graduates were sent to Rome, collections were formed, and a great deal of instructional material was assembled. In other words, it had adopted the classic system which had long been in force abroad.

This late beginning had had the advantage of saving Spain from an official policy, under which the whole country would have moved in the same direction. Local schools had been able to exist, and to maintain divergent trends. The Academy with its prestige and privileges must

have hastened the end of this situation, without deliberately setting out to do so. It was rather hoped that a centralising organisation might have been able to save Spanish art from its provincialism and help it to reach a level of international dialogue attractive to those social classes interested in the widest possible network of information. We feel like this even today, and art is centred on capital cities, not on towns and villages. For this reason artists turn towards one metropolis or another, and this in its turn becomes a world centre or remains a satellite. It is perhaps a bad thing, but it is a reality.

The Spanish art world was first of all Flemish, then Neapolitan, and finally—once these influences, political in origin, had been abandoned —turned towards Rome, following the example of Paris. It became dedicated to neo-classicism in the hope of achieving artistic unity (difficult for a country geographically divided by its mountains) and winning a place for Spanish art in the wider art world of Europe.

This was the task of the Academy of San Fernando and the other Academies that grew up in other Spanish cities; to promote art is in a sense to direct it. Official posts are offered to the masters, and a few jobs to the disciples; the building up of collections is encouraged, committing the injustices of which critics often speak. Thus the term "fine arts" could be justified in the official account books, rather than the simple heading "decorations and festivals".

Naturally, institutions never play any part in the evolution of painting, because though they can encourage fine arts, they obviously cannot manufacture geniuses.

Whatever the titles it confers and the courses it institutes, an Academy is tolerable only at a very modest level. Its importance comes out in the less obvious part of its work: the help it gives to unknown artists.

We need not take into account the aesthetic theories which the Academy taught in its courses, because they were at a purely theoretical level. We are interested in works. In fact, the Academy was not as orthodox as we might be tempted to believe. The organisation of the Academy soon became tossed by conflicting winds. If we look in the archives we find that Raphael Mengs was not the implacable director that he was supposed to be. All the rejections of the period were attributed to him, but in reality he was not the only one responsible. His suggestions were not always followed to the full. But under Mengs's direction the Academy was enriched by works which did not conform to the director's aesthetic ideas: drawings by Maratta, Domenichino, Lanfranco and Pier Leone Gozzi whose caricatures are similar to those of Tiepolo. Even when an Academy exists to serve certain ideas, it can still welcome their opposites. This did not prevent it from rejecting Goya.

In 1763 Goya had hoped to be awarded a scholarship; in vain. In 1766 he entered again. His hopes of success were greater because in the meantime Francisco Bayeu of Saragossa had joined the Academy. The theme for the competition was "the meeting at Burgos of Martha, Empress of Byzantium, with King Alfonso X the Wise. The Empress has come to seek the king's help in paying the ransom for her husband, the Emperor Baldwin II, who is a prisoner of the Egyptians. King Alfonso grants her the entire sum." It was a bewildering theme for contemporary artists; it remained to be seen whether a pupil could render visually a meeting between Byzantium and Castille in the 13th century. But it was not an exceptional theme if we consider that Francisco Bayeu in his various competitions had to represent the cruel Geryon, son of Callyroe and Chrysaor, attacking an Iberian. This was a monster with three heads and three bodies—we pity the painters whose masters were thus plunging them into the absurd. After the Byzantine-Castillian composition, Goya had to improvise in two hours on another theme, "the dispure of two noblemen, the Italian Giovanni da Urbino and the Spaniard Diego de Parades, as to which of them shall receive the insignia of the Marquis of Pescara"—another historical subject, because history was considered to be at the summit of the pictorial hierarchy. How could one show talent on such themes? Rubens might have been able to do it. Velasquez had painted the homage paid at the surrender of Breda, and Courbet was to show a similar scene. The ways by which one might reach the Royal Academy of painting must have seemed very difficult and anachronistic to someone who had hoped to make his way in art, having painted a few portraits and the apparition of the Virgin to St. James. Coming out of the examination and meeting in the streets girls in black mantillas, with slender figures and little feet peeping out from their long skirts, he must have thought that these were the proper themes for painting, not Burgos in the 13th century.

Why are academies founded? To offer to students the joy of painting? Would the joy of painting be achieved after the examination, or would the examination teach it? An academy, whatever the ideas of the founders and the members of the panel of judges may be, has to make a choice: it sets up obstacles and sees whether the candidates are capable of overcoming them. Goya put all his dedication and his technique into developing the theme he had been given, but he was not accepted. Francisco Bayeu's brother Ramon was 20 years old, like Goya. He too had entered the contest and received the gold medal.

Goya did not return to the Academy until 14 years later, and this time as an Academician. He had certainly found another way of getting into the Academy. As a young artist, they had not judged him to be ready; he was a provincial, and Luzan had certainly not been able to teach him all the aesthetic acrobatics in which artists had to engage: the historical and mythological knowledge necessary, and on top of that a technique which would enable him to deal with very tragic subjects. It is not surprising that he could not effectively depict a nobleman's dispute, or an Empress begging for her husband. None of the pictures we know would lead us to think that he would be at his best in vast historical and mythological themes. There is a record of a work called *Hercules at the feet of Omphale*, but this was a mere trifle. In examinations one could not appear to be trifling with the set theme. The works inspired by these themes have all disappeared through public indifference.

So Goya was unsuccessful, and gave up hope of getting the Prix de Rome, and there is no indication in the registers of the Academy that he ever tried again. He left for Rome alone and at his own expense. We know very little of this period in his life; legend tends to attribute to the artist the events befalling the characters in his pictures. Eugene d'Ors tells it in great detail: Goya found at dawn in a Madrid street with a knife stuck in his back, Goya going round Spain with a group of bullfighters, risking his life in village squares; Goya in Rome, climbing for a wager to the top of the Basilica of St Peter or scrambling over a convent wall and running away with a nun; Goya invited to the Court of St Petersburg, but refusing; Goya condemned to death by a Roman tribunal and freed by the intervention of a diplomat. If we look for the origin of these stories we find nothing, particularly not in the archives of notaries and registrars. But there is no need to believe only in official documents, and we cannot ignore all the events which do not appear in notaries' account-books and judges' pronouncements. We know little about either the beginning or the end of Goya's stay in Italy; we have only a letter in which he speaks of a picture entered in an examination for the Parma Academy in 1771. The themes was "Hannibal looks down on Italy from the Alps".

Another Academy, another examination, another failure. However, this was Parma, the city of Correggio and Parmigianino; the theme seemed less dismal than usual, and the judges were expecting a landscape with elephants in the style of Tiepolo. Goya's composition was never found. It probably exists in some Spanish or Italian collection under another artist's name. Anyway it is hard to trace even the picture of the winner, a certain Borroni. At least in this competition Goya's work received a mention. In the roll of honour we read: "The Academy mentions the work of Francisco Goya of Rome, pupil of F. Bayeu, painter to His Majesty the King of Spain. We noted a very subtle pictorial technique, warmth in Hannibal's expression and grandeur in his bearing. If the artist had been more truthful in his use of colour, and if the composition had kept closer to the theme, the artist would have won many votes." Borroni had been chosen unanimously. The competition is mentioned also in the *Mercure de France*, but the whole affair was soon forgotten, and no one suggested that Goya should remain in Italy. The members of the Parma Academy had mentioned four important features of Goya's composition: pictorial invention, facility of expression, feeling for colour that was expressive rather than faithful, and finally a lack of inclination to treat certain themes. Antiquity in Goya is limited to a few togas. He had no interest in details, whereas the judges insisted upon them in order to estimate the historical knowledge of the competitors. Even in a composition carried out so as not to surprise the judges too much, the painter revealed his own style and tendencies. Taking part in the contest for an Italian Academy, he hoped to get more from the Italians than from the Spanish. Unfortunately the difficulties were still there, because

a contest is launched to see whether a candidate is capable of carrying out a work foreign to his generation. Goya, beguiled by the official part of his work, had to overcome serious difficulties which were considered as conclusive proof of an artist's capabilities. Of course the younger generation cannot express itself on a subject which does not concern it; that is the result of the system, not of the generation gap.

In the register of the Parma Academy Goya is entered as a pupil of F. Bayeu, confirming an old bond which after various vicissitudes was to become a lasting collaboration, and in fact a family affair after Goya's marriage to his master's sister.

At the end of his Italian experience, Goya returned to Spain, to Saragossa, not Madrid. He very soon received commissions for murals, including the vault of the Church of Our Lady of the Pillar. It was the first fresco the artist had ever done, and the priests wanted to see whether he possessed the necessary technique. Goya first presented a preliminary sketch and then set to work. Looking at this work, it is interesting to see whether Goya had learned anything from his visit to Rome.

It is possible, considering that his first work had as its theme *The Adoration of the Name of Jesus*, a subject treated in the baroque style by Baciccia in the Church of Jesus in Rome. At Saragossa what was required was a composition in baroque style in keeping with the size and shape of paintings at the edges of the dome. It was a sort of compromise in the manner of Luca Giordano or Maratta, with many clouds, many cherubs, and above all an airy lightness which makes the ceiling disappear and gives the illusion of open sky and a heavenly pageant over the heads of the faithful. The ceiling had to give the faithful the sensation of the reality of the celestial world which everyone imagines in his prayers. Goya succeeded completely in this aim, as he later succeeded with the panels he painted for the chapel of the Charterhouse of the Aula Dei, in the suburbs of Saragossa. Although he used the *trompe l'oeil* technique, Goya did not keep to the content of the works of Italian artists in this field. Having accepted their formula, it was the interplay of light and mass which he applied with rare mastery, a proof that he had solved the problem of architectonic painting, the work that is done on a curved surface and transcends the visual field. But the spirit was not there, for despite the angels among the clouds, there is little of the celestial in his compositions. Space in his work is not meta-

physical and his characters belong to this earth. He shows them suspended in the air, but as though they were attached to balloons. It is true that they brandish the martyr's palm, lift their heads and open wide their arms towards the light falling from the lantern window, but ecstasy does not raise them from the ground. From his first religious work Goya reveals a feeling for the divine to which he remained faithful even twenty years later when he painted the cupola of San Antón de la Florida at Madrid. In the Saragossa' fresco which was a prelude to this other masterpiece, Goya showed his love for the masses, for rows of faces, for the presence of a crowd. While with the Italian artists figures soar with great ease to the four points of the compass, in Goya characters prefer to sit; they assemble in groups as though in a play. Space is occupied by close-knit groups between which more important characters are stationed. One would think that Goya rebelled against the Italian clarity which, in the darkness of hell or the radiance of paradise, in uncertainty and ecstasy, creates a space in which everyone feels free, in which every presence finds its place. Goya can make a composition, can give rhythm to a curved surface, link the lines of force one with another, achieve unity in a work that has to have an upward and a circular movement at one and the same time. But the artist is not satisfied with that; he has to repeat the man-oeuvre and improve on it. He contains the forces, tightens the groups, widens the gestures, and it was surely not Luzan who taught him these things; it was rather his stay in Italy.

The eye is attracted by details because the artist lingered over what was static, over what bound the painting to the vault, over everything that was actually there, whereas in this type of painting he was required to seek transparency above all. The light in his paintings gives no reflections, but shows up the depth of flesh. The angels are creatures full of mystery rather than beings infused with divine radiance. Goya does not exactly make it look like a masked ball, but he was more conscious of the wounded flesh of the martyrs or the naked arms of the female saints than of their transfiguration by the light of the divine presence.

This is the source of the great impact of these frescoes; the motif is Italian but played on different instruments. Think of Mozart played by a brass band, Mozart with a different sort of warmth, a different splendour, Mozart without lightness and elegance, a Mozart for peasants. Such was Goya at Saragossa. Madrid called him and Goya changed his tune: he was asked to paint boys playing, dogs barking—he who had painted the *Adoration of the Name of Jesus.* First they gave him a theme from ancient history, then he had to move on to everyday events, conventional events like the Byzantine-Castillian meeting of the 13th century. The conventional was what was asked for, and Bayeu's artists provided it.

Bayeu's art is much more mannered than Goya's. We have only to look at his frescoes in the Church of the Pillar and some studies for ceilings in the Prado. His studies had more in common with Tiepolo than his finished works, but the latter gave lightness to the walls even if in a conventional way. Bayeu had the required style and covered walls with thousands of celestial presences which were in reality his own individual creation. This is what distinguishes the masters: they cannot fulfil the tasks entrusted to them without to some extent impressing their own style upon them. His task with regard to Goya was completed. It was he who opened for him the gates of Madrid, and who had sensed his genius. The bonds became closer, but he could not have him awarded the scholarship to the Academy when his brother was also competing; however he married him to his sister Josefa, known as Pepa, who became pregnant at least twenty times but gave him only one living child. Goya painted a portrait of Pepa which shows discretion and kindness. Finally Bayeu recommended Goya to Mengs, and sent for him to Madrid.

When Goya spoke of his departure for the capital he said he had been invited by Mengs;

but Mengs was a stranger to him, and could only have known him through Bayeu. Besides, when Goya was in Italy he said Bayeu was his master. No one in Parma knew Bayeu, and that gave free rein to the admiration inspired by his pupil. In Spain, Goya preferred to give the great Flemish artist as his guarantor. He was, however, so remote from him that an approach could not have failed to annoy him. Trust the perception of artists, who know how to put aside whatever could be an obstacle to their work. In the case of Goya, the contradictory information he gives at intervals of a few years, his changeability, reveal a latent, deep-rooted conflict within himself.

In 1780–81 Goya and Bayeu were working together on the Church of the Pillar at Saragossa. Bayeu protested, in his capacity of teacher and man in charge: what his brother-in-law was painting seemed ugly and strident. Goya obeyed and corrected it. The archives contain no trace of the dispute between the two artists; they hint at the submission of the younger one, but the historians insist that he was humiliated. Everyone wants the hero to be always right; those who work with him are committing *lèse-majesté* when they contradict or hinder him.

Bayeu certainly had good reasons for arguing with Goya. Probably he would reproach him with the heaviness and earthly appearance of the saints; they were all that prevented the artist from fitting into his master's plan for the decora-tion. Bayeu was showing his professional conscience. Why did Goya have to disagree? The master guided the pupil, who followed him. The master had chosen him to carry out works inspired by a given conception of art, in conditions favourable to their execution. That Goya resisted, not in discussion, but with plans prejudicial to the whole complex of the decoration, confirms a disagreement. Bayeu noticed in this painter an almost unconscious inner resistance, but it did not cause a break. Fifteen years later, in 1795, when Goya was fifty and Bayeu over sixty, he painted the master's portrait. Bayeu amazed his contemporaries by the glacial appearance he succeeded in assuming. Goya succeeded in reproducing this appearance exactly: the lapels of the grey coat are closed like armour; a face above a breastplate, a stormy, tyrannical face; and a brush pointing downwards almost like a lowered weapon. Fifteen years after the quarrel in church over the frescoes, Goya saw his brother-in-law and master as a solitary and still dangerous man; he respected him but no longer feared him. Goya could yield to his commands, but he was one of those whom nothing could shake. Gentle in appearance, but physically tough, he had the characteristics of a man destined to live long. Those fated to die young are intransigent; probably Goya had a presentiment that he was destined for a long life. He could let things slide or devote himself to

Portrait of F. Bayeu,
Prado, Madrid, 1795

tasks that others might consider a waste of time. Goya had vast reserves of time to waste. He gave them to Bayeu, to the priests of Saragossa, to the successive kings of Spain, to the Academy of San Fernando. Bayeu had bound him to himself by being more powerful. Goya never wearied of these submissions, and his reserves of strength were astonishing. He accomplished a second life's work, hidden in the heart of the first, and his two careers were closely interwoven. Clearly Bayeu used Goya, but he raised him to a social level which allowed him to fulfil himself. At Saragossa Goya would have made his way by confining himself to opposing the baroque in church painting. At Madrid he met no more obstacles at the Academy which had rejected him as a young artist, but he had other problems.

The evolution of an artist depends on the aesthetic questions which are current in his times. In painting as in biology, no observation is valid if it does not take into account the living conditions of the cell being analysed. At Madrid, Goya had to face the arguments of his times. Without them he would have come to a halt. His first employment, unfortunately, found him at the Tapestry Factory.

In the first work he did, he gave way to convention; but his inspiration dried up, which is so obvious that the first five tapestry cartoons done in 1775 were not considered to be by the artist until documentary proof was discovered.

It is difficult not to impute this failure to his incapacity to master a new technique. His cartoons were always simply paintings, impossible to transfer to tapestry. But what Goya painted for the Tapestry Factory was similar to what the Bayeu brothers or Jean de Castillo painted, and in fact to everything created in the various tapestry workshops of Europe. After the Second World War some 15th century wallhangings were rediscovered, and the art was revived with its proper technique, that is to say taking into account the fact that the picture must be translated into weaving. Historians of tapestry gloss over the 18th century and harshly criticise the 19th in which there was complete confusion between painting and tapestry, going as far as portraits. The arts of tapestry and painting were never separated, and the crisis of the 18th century was not a break, a separation between two conceptions, but a common evolution. When the monumental and tragic themes of the preceding centuries had been abandoned, the art of tapestry found itself unprovided for when its motifs were expressed with purely pictorial criteria. Painting has thus become less and less suitable for translation into weaving.

At the Prado 39 paintings, divided between three rooms, bear witness to Goya's concepts of tapestry, but there is certainly no question of being able to transfer them to weaving. The sketches have been put into gilt frames which fit in perfectly with the furnishings of the rooms, and are to be preferred to the sometimes unfaithful copies made by the tapestry weavers of Santa Barbara.

The presentation does not take account of the chronological order—they are works carried out from 1776 to 1791, a period in which Goya worked mainly for the Factory, but they are the only works for tapestry which the Museum possesses. Of the cartoons in question the best are the oldest ones, with the exception of the first five which have been attributed to F. Bayeu, Vandergoten, Ramon Nayeu, and Gonzalez Velasquez, that is to say, to a trend rather than to an artist. Today they are easily attributable to Goya. The presentation, the density of the brush-strokes at that time seem to indicate more inexperience than power. A year later the cartoons show greater mastery. More than any other artist of the Factory, Goya was sensitive to the contrast of light and shade. This sensitivity is not required for tapestry, because walls need lightness, a gradation of tones for the clouds, an airy mass of foliage, but above all as little shade as possible. Light must not create contrasts but be diffused. The only contrasts are between colours, in such a way that the tapestry becomes a wall of wool. Goya's personal style in tapestries is one in which great dark masses contrast with soft clear tones, in which light shines on these dark masses.

His interpretations of tapestry techniques appear in all their variations when we compare his sketches with the tapestries taken from them; better still when we compare the initial picture with the finished tapestry. To do this we have to go from the Prado to the Escorial. In a dining room at the Escorial we see Goya tapestries hung on the walls in uninterrupted succession. The decoration, by Goya and the Bayeu brothers or Castillo, shows no gaps of any kind, because the decorator had precedence over the artists, who had to supply him with decoration rather than original works, so that the decorator could make use of them to complete his work.

La Novillada,
Prado, Madrid, 1780

Consider for example a cartoon like *A Walk in Andalusia;* it shows a wood in which men are walking with their faces hidden in their cloaks. The only uncovered face is that of a woman in an elaborate dress. Shadows are everywhere, in the folds of the cloaks and under the wide sombreros. A few hints of colour here and there: this is Goya's sketch.

On the basis of this plan, the tapestry work is remarkable: light tones have been added wherever possible. The earth has been lightened, the size of the trees reduced and some removed, the rocks have been lightened and plants added in the foreground, giving shape to what were only splashes of colour.

Another tapestry, *Spring*, which is shown at the Prado under the name of *The Flower-girls* is another example: a kneeling girl is offering a flower to another girl holding a child by the hand, while a peasant behind her is trying to frighten her, holding a rabbit in one hand and signalling to passers-by, with a finger on his lips, not to say he is there. The sketch (Duke of Montellano Collection, Madrid) is powerful and very colourful; the colours combine silver and black tones shot through with blue highlights. There is a red coat of an intense colour, and traces of dark leaves on the ground. When we see at the Prado the cartoon taken from the sketch we wonder whether this cartoon was also painted by Goya. There are the same trees, the same characters, but the work has been lightened, and now pink and pale blue predominate, and there is yellow where in the sketch there was red and flesh tints. And the characters are no longer those conceived by the artist, but look as though they had just left the hands of a theatrical costumier. The clothes are well pressed, and the shawl comes to a neat point at the back; only the man's moustache and hair do not seem to have been retouched. Goya did not usually bother with these details in his works. The expressions have become conventional whereas at first they were fresh and spontaneous. The heads are more bowed, the movements seem like those of an actor reciting a speech, the gestures are wider, as though a theatrical producer had suggested them. Was Goya the costumier and the producer? It could have been an adviser at the Factory, unless it was Goya himself with someone guiding his hand.

F. Bayeu 1734–1795—*The Walk of Delights,*
Tapestry cartoon,
Prado, Madrid

The Fair of Madrid,
Prado, Madrid, 1779

Comparing the first cartoons (1776) with the last (1791) we notice that the painter has softened and moved towards light colours, which were also what was required for the decorative function which the artistic product had to fulfil. We see an example of this change in the cartoon which shows a man carried by two others in the setting of a building site. The bearers have very serious expressions, even for the subject of the cartoon, *The Wounded Mason*, but there is also a sketch in which the bearers are laughing and the title is *The Drunken Mason*. The two works are exactly the same except for the expressions on the two faces. We may imagine Goya asking: "Do you want the bearers happy or sad, or do you not approve of the sight of drunkenness?" Goya would never have asked questions like this at the beginning, but by now he had probably learnt a great deal and could adapt himself.

We are tempted to say that the artist's particular charm lies in the dark pictures: *La Novillada, The Crockery Seller, The Blind Guitarist, The Fair at Madrid* (in reality a scene in a large flea-market), *Dinner on the Grass, Open-air Dance at San Antón de la Florida*, while in the lighter-coloured pictures he was a slave to the demands of others. We could compile a whole list of protests against courts: even Zurbaran, like Goya, was obliged to paint historical subjects like *The Defence of Cadiz Against the English* or *The Labours of Hercules*, giving up his preference for mystical painting. Goya was a victim like other artists.

How can we explain his continual efforts to reach the summit of the hierarchy of court painters? Certainly Goya needed money, and in his letters he stresses the satisfaction of being able to earn a comfortable living with his brush. If he was dissatisfied with his job, he could have left it and earned his living with portraits and religious paintings. Objectively we have to admit that not all his dark cartoons are a complete success, and that not all the light ones are ugly or conventional, even though the artist was obliged to make them satisfy his customers. Looking at the works of this period we have to admit that Goya, at the end of his period of work at the Factory, did not have a unified style. He could paint a family portrait, neat and smooth, with fixed expressions like wax figures, as fashion required, and a few weeks later a religious scene with a Zurbaranesque gravity, or a scene reeking of sulphur and full of strange lights, in which a crucifix throws sparks at a dying man already menaced by the powers of hell. Goya's art became more and more powerful, lively and vigorous. But Goya also painted jolly little scenes with a merry group playing blind man's buff. Between *The Dance* of 1777 and *Blind Man's Buff* of 1791 there is no difference of theme. It is a party in the open air. The difference is that whereas in the first there is only joy, in the second, despite the smiles, there is also unease. The first is simply a festival, the second, in its spacious setting, is an invitation to reflect on the human condition. The time was to come when he could no longer be the painter of these puppets; the storm had blown them away. But until the moment when he plunged into tragedy, the artist had worked on many different themes.

He gave the Factory town and country scenes, scenes common to all artists, like the four seasons, children's games, hunting parties, card games, brawls in front of inns; in fact, chronicles of popular life which the prince wanted to admire on his palace walls. Before that the demand was for allegory and mythology, divinities who could be shown as swans or bulls—and this demand prevailed throughout Europe, at all the courts. Spain was more original in wanting the royal palace to be decorated with national legends. Two Italian artists at Madrid under King Philip IV, Procaccini and Sani, had composed a series of tapestries on the story of Don Quixote. Sani, who died in 1772, had specialised in popular scenes, with beggars and charlatans, thus maintaining the realism of the 17th century, which Velasquez had brought to the royal palace, rather than the fascination of Latin and Greek mythology.

In the 18th century popular tradition spread everywhere: to Venice with Zuccarelli, to Paris with Jouy's tapestries woven from the cartoons of J. B. Huet; a whole small regional world, showing town-dwellers the joys of washing clothes in the stream, drinking a glass at the inn, dancing in the village square, picking fruit or cutting corn. This display of the happiness of the poor, intended for the rich, may seem surprising, but not if we take into account the communication between social classes studied in the plays of Beaumarchais, and the nostalgia for the country in town-dwellers possessing country houses where, besides silence, they sought the song of the birds, new-laid eggs, fresh milk and a sense of balance which the town could not give. It is an old nostalgia, going back to Horace and Virgil; in Paris in the 17th century, you could see the dance "Country Wedding" being performed. It was invented by the court musician Jean Hoteterre.

In these folk scenes there is no attempt to find a reason for living; it is a world with immutable laws, governed by the seasons, and so without surprises or dangers. Even the farm-workers' fights are like a ballet. Popular painting is distinct from realism and mythological painting. If Goya paints the snow falling on poor people it is an image of winter softened by the fact that summer is bound to follow.

Goya brought into painting for tapestry, dominated at one time by heroic or Biblical scenes, the same kind of themes as the Bayeu brothers. His work is plastically richer, but creates problems in transferring it to wool. By subsequently painting large sections in light colours, the transference was made easier, and the arrangement of the colours made possible that unity of surface in which the art of weaving consists. The original difficulty of transfer resulted in works in which details were more important than the whole. These were betrayals which did not worry Goya very much. When the tapestries were completed, his cartoons were rolled up and stored in basements. They were found in 1869 among 255 sketches showing the work done by painters at the Factory. The fate of cartoons was a curious one: as soon as they were reproduced they were laid aside because their function was to guide the weaver's hand, while today they are preferred to the tapestries themselves.

Should these works be considered as simply functional, or as an important stage in Goya's career? For Goya, as for other artists, we have to consider technique, size, and subjects set. The artists had to accept subjects for which they were not naturally suited, but it often happened that this side-tracking of their genius did not weaken them but enabled them to carry out works of the first order on subjects which at first glance seemed a deplorable distortion. Goya decorated the bedrooms of the Infantas of the Asturias, and dining rooms at the Prado. The artist had access in this way to a world of fair maidens and rough *hidalgos* which he never gave up. He even painted *majas* on the walls of his house, the Quinta del Sordo. He showed one terrorised by a coven of witches around a great he-goat, and another watching by a tomb. The clear bright style he had used to depict the figures of aristocratic little girls playing *galina ciega* (blind man's buff) also served for portraits of girls and young women. In decorative work he was sure of being able to paint festivals and make the shoulders and arms of beautiful ladies look like mother-of-pearl. It is the pleasantest part of his work, constant, and yet modified from time to time like a sweet song which is deliberately accompanied by howls and screams. When he was not told precisely that his work was intended for a girl's room or a dining-hall, he preferred to paint less civilized festivals, amusements concentrating the entire human personality, which—still respecting the rules—appealed to his instincts.

In moving from tapestry cartoons to other art forms he was able to abandon the use of bright colours. It must have been pleasant for him to return to using dark colours among which the silks and satins of the clothes traced silver sparks. This happens in the *Portrait of the Court of Floridablanca,* stiff as a Mengs, but set aflame by the red of the coat. He must have had great pleasure in achieving a balance between the luminous reflections, the splashes of colour without outlines, and the gradual passage from dark to light which was impossible to obtain in tapestry and which made the picture intensely vibrant. He followed the same procedure in the religious pictures which he painted in 1786 in the Convent of San Antón at the Prado, and in 1787 at the Convent of Santa Anna at Valladolid, meditative, contemplative, silent works. He used this quivering colour in the *Portrait of the Marquesa de Pontejo* in which the great lady is caught in her delicate and complex costume as though in a trap, and looks sadly at the painter from afar, and the sadness is scarcely lessened by her roses and ribbons. He uses it in the *Portrait of the Osuna family;* the head of the family had asked him to carry out the decoration of his house. In this case too, the colour is not rigidly confined; it is free in the transparent laces, the light tulle of the dresses, the highlights of the coats; it trembles in the band of light sweeping over the background.

But did Goya assert himself only in details and never in the complete work? We have studied his work on the vaults of the church of Saragossa, on the altars of the churches of Valladolid and Madrid, in the decoration of royal apartments and on the walls of aristocrats' drawing-rooms. Here he continues the baroque tradition, there the style of the Tapestry Factory; elsewhere he follows the vaporous stillness of Zurbaran, the rigidity of the portraits of Mengs. In every case he showed remarkable personal gifts, including an exceptional vigour in the composition of large areas of light and shade, a taste for the most subtle and intimate vibrations of colour, and a sense of grouping. His power, escaping from the rules of classical balance, attains the dynamism of the baroque, but always with signs of borrowing. We wonder therefore if he had died at 40 in 1786 when he was appointed court painter, could we have considered him a master?

The artist who had produced cartoons like *The Crockery Seller, La Novillada, The Walk in Andalusia*, the frescoes of the Charterhouse of the Aula Dei, and the cupolas of the Church of the Pillar at Saragossa, was a master. In the cartoon *The Parasol* he had created an image which could become a symbol of Spanish life.

However, even though his talent was above that of all the other artists of the Court, even though he represented the vitality of Spanish art in the second half of the 18th century, he had not yet reached the level to which he later attained, and which gives his work an international intellectual status to which painters in every country subscribe. In 1786 it could be said of him that he was a Hogarth not fully developed. Think of the precocity of Bonnington, dead at 26, of whom Delacroix said that he was like a king in his field. At forty, Goya was a remarkable painter who had outshone his contemporaries, and reached a prominent position, probably the dominant position in his country. At that time, however, he was not one of those artists whose name the painters of today pronounce with awe, and who have carried the arts to the level of the greatest human adventures: Rembrandt, Beethoven, Michelangelo, Leonardo da Vinci, Victor Hugo, Goethe.

When Goya gained his entry into official circles it did not mean only that he was considered fit to carry out the king's orders, but meant also that he could look at the royal collections and discover Velasquez, the exemplary servant of the court, whose example he had to follow and from whom he had to learn that he could develop his own talent while still serving the king. Certainly Velasques interested him, and he began to make etchings of his predecessor's work. Three of his etchings have been preserved: a *Flight into Egypt*, a *St Francis of Paula*, and a *St Isidore*. Goya at once showed great mastery, while Rembrandt at the beginning was hesitant, because he was working alone while Goya had a master. Goya's works are the fruit of a certain aesthetic concept followed consistently, and they have the coldness of school exercises, except for the *St Isidore*, which looks as though it were carried out when the master was not looking. It is less elaborate than the others, but the saint, with his eyes raised to heaven and his arms flung wide, prefigures the famous image of a man thrown to the ground by the revelation of the divine presence, an image which Goya was to carry out twenty years later in the *Caprichos*. His first unfinished essay showed, even though imprecisely, his taste for intense blacks and for features merely sketched in. In 1778 he began to make engravings after Velasquez. The Velasquez-Goya encounter is exciting and gave rise to seven large pictures (the second one, *Los Borrachos*—the drunkards— measures 39 x 29 cm) which, together with the lithographs, are the largest size prints the artist ever made. The original format is smaller, as the six other prints prove, and in them the artist uses a new technique, aquatint, combining this technical curiosity with the large format.

The work he did is of varying quality; the serious portraits are a good interpretation of the work of Velasquez, although not very personal. Other works, like *Las Meninas*, show carelessness in the execution of details, especially faces, while we can see how Goya had examined and reproduced the framing of the doors and windows (in front of which Velasquez painted his characters) with a painter's curiosity. It is clearly the work of someone skilled in construction. Perceiving the contrast between the Infanta in a light colour and her attendant dwarf in a dark one, he let the white paper show through in his copy of the princess's dress, cutting deep into the copper plate to obtain the strong black which he needed to emphasise the contrast. Goya appears even more as the engraver in his version of the dwarfs and the figures of Aesop and Menippus. Probably there was someone supervising his work, or else Goya was already employed by the king or was attempting to become so, and dared not forget the respect due to royalty.

Comparing the pictures of Velasquez with

Goya's etchings we can see the differences: Goya
must have been faced with similar problems to
those of the tapestry weavers when they had to
transfer his cartoons to their work, as in the
case when he had to engrave a hat with a white
plume against the sky.

Among the works of Velasquez assembled in
the New Palace at Madrid, what did he choose?
He turned towards the early realistic works,
accentuating the realism of the *Borrachos*. The
abstract, inorganic nature of the character's
back, which in Velasquez slightly resembles
Michelangelo, becomes in Goya a massive
peasant's back in a rumpled coat. The features
are marked, the wrinkles deepened, the liveliness
of the eyes increased. Goya has followed the
broad lines of the picture, the alternation of open
and closed space, the tormented and angular
play of light in this mysterious composition.
Naturally Goya was more at his ease in the
transcription of the portraits. Goya later remembered that Velasquez had included self-
portraits in his pictures and followed his example
in the portrait of the family of Charles IV, showing himself in the shadows behind his august
models, in a new, complex arrangement. For this
he placed his models in a line, because in studying Velasquez, Goya studied not only his genius,
but also the tricks which could help a court
painter. When he engraved the portraits of
Philip III, Philip IV, Prince Baltaser Carlos,

Queen Margaret and Queen Isabel, the Infante Fernando and the minister Olivares, Goya, who had not yet had the chance to paint the king and the royal family, and was the second assistant at the Tapestry Factory, may have thought he might one day be able to paint kings, princes, queens and the minister Godoy. We do not know if that was so: it is certain that Goya later succeeded by following the example of Velasquez. Goya also learned that a court painter had to amuse the onlookers with his pictures, and so he engraved the kind of portraits of buffoons, dwarfs and the vagabond-philosophers that we find in all Spanish art from Velasquez to Picasso. At the Prado there are two copies of these pictures, two painted copies which could be by Goya, proving that Goya studied his master brush in hand. Velasquez demanded this analysis through the study of colour, and Goya, admiring him, learned that it was possible to be a great painter even using conventional formulas. The study of Velasquez encouraged him to this submission, making him realise that independence can be found in any aspect of banality. And Goya knew how to find it.

Anyway, he was only expected to continue the work of Velasquez, because kings demand to be represented as their ancestors were; only thus can they feel themselves to be real sovereigns. The tradition of equestrian portraits is very ancient and perhaps goes back to the time when the horseman first felt superior to the man on foot. In Roman times artists made two kinds

of busts, the official and the private; in the same
way painters showed kings not only as horsemen
but in their moments of relaxation. Louis XIV
wished to appear a king even when dressing;
but the figure of the saint-king—Charlemagne,
Louis IX of France—did not last long.

There was no simplicity in the Spanish
sovereigns, only resignation to the progressive
debasing of their function as kings by divine
right, and an indifference as to whether the
image of majesty were revived or not. The
decoration of their palaces did not have to be
dedicated to their glory; it was enough that it
should be pleasant and edifying. From artists
they wanted diverting pictures; and for their
children's education, they wanted scenes stimu-
lating good Catholics to charity and not Spaniards to supremacy. Unlike these European
sovereigns, Napoleon revived the trend that
from Maximilian of Austria to Louis XIV of
France had demanded that artists should glorify
the monarch. But he was alone: absolute
monarchs blushed to be shown as absolute
masters because they were no longer the agents
of God on earth and did not like to see their own
triumph. This respectable modesty did not
prevent their defeat.

Goya, studying Velasquez, realised that he
could take his place, and he learned from this
single model what his functions demanded of
him. He took up the same themes, even if they
had nothing to do with royalty, like that of the
spinners.

Family of Charles IV,
Prado, Madrid, 1800

The Sermon of St. Bernardine,
San Francisco el Grande, Madrid, 1782–1783

Portrait of Sebastian Martinez,
Metropolitan Museum of Art, New York, 1792

This submission lasted for a long time, so that one might say there were two Goyas, one official and the other clandestine. The conditions in which he found himself point to this division, but it is difficult to believe that an artist can really divide himself in two.

These two series of works by Goya are equally rich, because we find the signs of his genius both in the record of things seen (men and festivals) and in imaginative works. Spanish society demanded portraits: dukes, duchesses, aristocratic girls and great ladies. On the back of the profile of King Charles III's brother Don Luis, the painter wrote: "Painted on September 11th, from 9 to 12 in the morning". Faced with this rush of customers demanding portraits, Goya succeeded in satisfying them. Noblemen received him in society, and bankers imitated them. He showed them small, seated behind enormous tables, as though overwhelmed by their functions, but they did not argue, because he was the artist who coped with all their demands. He agreed to paint the great lady in the wilderness—a tract of wild countryside—or the baby with its toys. He lived among men and painted them, even putting his own portrait into the large picture of the sermon of St Bernadine for an altar of the Church of St Francis the Great at Madrid. He is there in his proper place, a witness to the men and women of his time, a worthy successor to Velasquez.

Goya was at the service of his contemporaries, with perfect mental and social balance; but he very soon decided to move in another direction, towards unusual festivities, crimes and surging crowds. It seems impossible to pass from one art to another in which creatures are no longer considered as a physical presence, but through their actions. It means the mobilisation of new forces, the exploration of an unknown world,

and the same artist passing from the artistic themes of the court to artistic themes which later formed the subject of psychoanalytical studies.

Historians attribute this turning point to changes in the artist's physical constitution. In 1793, after months of violent headaches, Goya became completely deaf. Deaf persons are thought to develop greater visual acuity. If we look at one of the works carried out a little before his illness, the *Portrait of Sebastian Martinez* (Metropolitan Museum, New York) we see that the composition has an exceptional visual sensitivity. It is the subtlety of the eye which Goya developed in himself. The reflections of sunlight on a blue silk coat with white stripes are achieved with a strength such as had never previously appeared, and the colour in this picture becomes an ever-changing play of light, a foretaste of the manner of the Impressionists who came later. Now let us consider another portrait, the *Portrait of Doctor Peral* National Gallery, London) and we shall see that the artist is less concerned with these subtleties, because what he is seeking above all is the expression. It seems as though Goya, no longer hearing what people say, is obsessed by their silence, and tries harder than before to make them express their thoughts in their faces. It seems as though Goya, deprived of the normal standards by which the five senses give the total image of the person, no longer wishes to affirm the supremacy of sight over the other senses, and toning down his palette, is now moving towards dark colours. He wants to render the expression in the density of form, the violence of gesture, the contraction of the face, rather than by colour. It was a crisis which plunged Goya into a world that was silent but discordant, full of shouts and dissonances, a world that screams without sound. When it

does not scream, Goya does not perceive it. If one of the five senses is lost, do they all have to deteriorate? Art has its deaf musicians, from Beethoven to Fauré, its blind poets like Homer, and those maimed like Hartung who have attained to a tranquil intuition of the universe. Is it perhaps a factor that can transform an artist at the service of eager sitters into a solitary man, obsessed with discord, disharmony and excess? Goya went through a painful crisis, but let us not forget that the greater part of his work dates from this disablement. He had already worked for 22 years and he had still 35 left, and he went on painting trifles and happy portraits as well. In fact he painted more of them, and gave them greater impact; in other words the style he had chosen remained very much alive, and even showed a dynamic evolution. The crisis of his deafness can be considered as a turning-point in his career, a moment at which he began to seek more actively the tactile values of painting and to accept the burden of people and things which he had hitherto avoided. Two years after this crisis Francisco Bayeu died and Goya took his place as director of the painting section of the Academy of San Fernando. His new post and deafness certainly gave him greater consciousness of himself and his independence. Without this official promotion Goya would not have undertaken his second career within the first. It was these events that gave rise to the works in which he ceased to look at people only in their Court dress, their theatrical peasant costume, or their amusements in the arena and their sacred rites on church ceilings. He looked at them now from a different point of view—that of crime and madness; he painted them from the other aspect of life, which up to now he had avoided—cruelty.

Chapter IV

TOWARDS CRUELTY AND THE MACABRE

Goya's entry into the world of cruelty is the logical outcome of the picturesque scenes which he composed for the royal tapestries. In a series of small pictures which were sold to the same Marquis of Osuna who had posed with his wife and four children for a family portrait four years earlier, we see a new feeling of violence. Not the heroic violence of battle, but pure, unjustified violence. There is a shooting—nothing heroic, no regiments manoeuvring face to face, but soldiers letting off their guns at a woman who is fleeing, carrying her baby in her arms. There is a huge fire, and in the glow we see no acts of courage, but a hysterical crowd. passing semi-naked bodies from hand to hand. There is the beheading of a man, and there is a shipwreck on a rocky shore; we see no rescuers appearing on the horizon and no ship-wrecked mariners kneeling to thank the Lord. There is a woman thrown to the ground by a man who is trying to cut her throat. There is a naked woman in the hands of brigands in the depths of a cave. These are not the misfortunes of Justine, but they are subjects which could fascinate others who, like Goya's contemporary the Marquis de Sade, are interested in those who suffer for virtue.

These pictures were painted to form a series, and probably tell the story of a heroine who had seized the public imagination, or else they are illustrations for fashionable romances. Historians have not been able to decide. The first years of the 19th century were rich in similar works: we remember Gericault's drawings illustrating the phases of the assassination of the magistrate Fualdès, and his portrayal of a hanging. These scenes of violence certainly had a strange effect when these pictures, in which genre painting found new life, were hung on the wall.

The themes on which these pictures are based
are the classic ones of terror. I was recently
leafing through periodicals in which novels by
Dumas, Féval and Ponson du Terrail were
published in instalments, and their illustrations
were all inspired by fear. The fear is born when
the elements and the instincts are unleashed,
when a force rages unchecked, when the normal
balance is overthrown, when daylight becomes
deep night. It is born of the moments in which
thought follows secret paths to communicate
with forces that turn away from the divine will
and the established order. It was when he was
painting his first violent series that Goya first
became interested in witchcraft; and pictures like
the *Witches' Sabbath* at the Galliano Museum
(Madrid) or the *Devil's Lamp* (National Gallery,
London) are the prelude to the mysterious

The Shooting,
Marques de la Romana Collection, Madrid, 1794–1795

Géricault 1791–1824—*Sketch for the Fualdés Affair,*
Museum, Lille, 1817

Tauromaquia,
Juanito Apiniani

El Cid

The Hunt of the Bull

The Devil's Lamp,
National Gallery, London, 1798

paintings which followed 25 years later on the walls of his country house. It will be said that witchcraft scenes are not found in Velasquez; in about 1788 Goya had painted a series of eight pictures on the subject of bullfighting. In the same period, but in a large format and in a style recalling the tapestry cartoons, he had shown an incident called *Attack on the Stagecoach* (Duke of Montellano Collection, Madrid). The sketch for the cartoon *The Field of San Isidro* is in the same style.

The Bullfight, The Attack on the Stagecoach and *The Picnic of all Madrid at San Isidro* are all pictures which tell a story or record an event. It matters little whether they are happy or sad; they show the kind of things which people gossip about in the streets, in taverns and in drawing-rooms; they are public events. It is a style familiar to Velasquez who, in the *View of Saragossa*, shows horsemen, orange-sellers and aristocratic ladies taking the air while they wait for the arrival of girls with lace parasols, dressed in white. Velasquez had not yet painted the hunts of King Philip IV.

Goya continued to record events in this way, proper to a court painter. But how did this traditional style, preserved by Horace Vernet

The Death of the Picador,
Cotnareanu Collection, New York, 1788

Expulsion of the people from the arena before the
bullfight,
Private collection, Paris

Bullfight,
Marquesa de la Torrecida Collection, Madrid

Banderilleros,
Private collection, Paris

The Bullring,
Cardona Collection, Madrid

Witches' Sabbath,
Prado, Madrid, about 1819–1823

when he painted Napoleon's hunts, change into Goya's tragic and fantastic style?

Towards the end of the 18th century the social and cultural view of life was beginning to pass from a detached view of events to one that was passionately involved. In a fight we no longer see the harmonious, almost ballet-like meeting of two opponents; we can now feel the presence of death. There was an obsession with crime, particularly with murder. Everyone discovered a more serious reality, and became aware of the drama of life. They realised that they were walking on a volcano, and it is this volcano that is before our eyes.

The theme of the bullfight is a popular one which we find in Venice as early as the 16th century in the pictures of Heintz the younger, but it is an amusement not far removed from the royal hunts. In Spain the *corrida*, which the Cid Campeador is said to have started, has become a ritual the outcome of which is almost pre-ordained; its phases come in orderly sequence. In his first series of *Tauromaquia* Goya treated the various *tercios* as *aficionados* that is, without any imaginative addition to the record, and the specialists can list the actions and phases of the fight shown in the picture. The bull can be followed from birth, through training on a

country farm, to death in the arena; the series of pictures tells us what a great festival the *corrida* is.

It is a chronicle in which Goya rises above himself: for example, in the *Death of the Picador* (New York), the event is recorded in all its tragedy. The bull is a black sinister mass. The beast is carrying the picador on its head transfixed by a horn, and hurling itself at the horse which the other picador is spurring towards it. On the stands, the figures of the spectators are motionless blotches. We are now far from the agitation seen in an earlier episode when the spectators had been asked to leave the arena so that the fight could go on, and Goya depicted this agitation with bright, vivid brush-strokes. Then the spectators were a vibrant mass; here they are rigid because the cruelty of the scene paralyses them. Even death is part of a show.

There is the same tragic atmosphere in the scene where a woman prostrate on the ground, a knife at her throat, is about to be killed, and is screaming with terror. Murderers, corpses, rapists, could thus penetrate into the most intimate rooms of great houses, and be hung on the wall beside the traproom fights of Wouwerman and Brouwer, and Teniers's drawings of monkeys; their intention was to amuse, because fantasy and caprice were not considered foolish in those days. Everyone had the right to dream about impossible scenes, and to wonder at strange tastes. The psychoanalytical key did not yet exist, and to explore the subconscious in this way was a new adventure.

The painter also asks us to look kindly on his themes. In one of his letters in which he speaks of his new themes he writes: "I have painted these pictures to occupy my imagination, which is tormented by all the ills that afflict me. They are the record of observations that cannot be made in commissioned pictures, which do not favour imagination and invention."

Imagination and invention: the witches carrying homunculi in their baskets are an entertainment. Goya amused himself by depicting scenes which the modern dramatist Arrabal considers terrifying. He liked popular themes and wanted to surround himself with them in the decoration of his own house. Not only for their folklore interest, but because this was a means of arriving at a higher truth through a series of frightening images. In the ceremonial of devil-worship he had access to the dark face of the world; hitherto he had shown only its bright face, in his decorations for the bedrooms of the Infantes.

Even the theme of witchcraft is not new; in the Prado there are about forty pictures by Teniers the Younger, bought by Elizabeth Farnese for La Granja, and by Charles IV for Aranjuez. The taste for these pictures was due to the influence of a governor from Flanders during the reign of Philip IV. Goya saw these works in the royal palace. He liked in them either the Flemish aspect (bivuoacs, kitchens, surgical operations and smoke-rooms) or the mysterious side (alchemists at their furnaces, flights of monsters inherited from Bosch which appear in the *Temptations of St Anthony*). There was nothing to cause panic in these *diableries* and scenes of the people. Teniers were not Callot, and his messengers from hell were as amusing as the buffooneries of the monkeys which he showed writing books or making music. It was a type of fantasy which allowed the painter to depict terrible scenes of cruelty, smoothing the path to complete liberty in painting. In fantasy and caprice all is permitted, because it is the artist who is the master, not needing to give an account of himself to anyone, except when he paints a crime or a Black Mass, and then he is responsible to the devil. They were beginning to play a dangerous game, and the images that were being used were not as tame as one might think.

"When you need me, come after midnight to the Bridge of the Manzanares, clap your hands three times and you will see black horses appear." This sentence is not by Cazotte or the brothers Grimm, or Novalis or Tieck or Goethe, but by a typical 18th century gentleman, a man of logic and science, believing in scientific technique, who became an engineer and an inventor of machines, while also studying ethnology and prehistory, who travelled as an archaeologist, and was welcomed in the embassies of distant lands, and who also published novels. The sentence is by a kind of man not very different from the Frenchman Vivant Denon. It is by a Pole who committed suicide in 1815 at the age of 54, Jan Potocki. This Pole published in French at St Petersburg a huge book recently brought to light by Roger Caillois, which also inspired a Polish director to make a film called *The Manuscript found at Saragossa*. We are quoting this book because it represents the taste the period for the fantastic and the occult in entertainment. The "Spanish manuscript" is said to have been found by a captain of the guard during the siege of Saragossa by Napoleon. Made up of a series of ten adventures, it is a kind of Decameron taking place between the Sierra Morena and Madrid. In the book there are figures of gipsies of whose adventurous lives Teniers had told. In Potocki there are cannibals, but less powerful than the Jews and Cabalists. All peoples outlawed by race or thought meet in the wilderness, appear and disappear, and bring about fantastic sights in Spanish mountain inns. Here is the home of the new world—or what would today be called the anti-world. A frequent theme in the book is that of the two hanged men drying in the wind. The wayfarer dreams of lying with two Moslem ladies who love him, and awakens among the bones of the two fleshless skeletons. There is in the book a macabre eroticism, a persistent desire for love, an all-pervading diabolical way of life. The author knows the infinite power of even low-ranking demons. The devil does not leave his followers long to enjoy the happiness offered them before bringing them back to the most horrifying subjection.

The demon world, in the book and for Potocki, has a literary element. This devil, so much talked about in the Middle Ages, is no longer believed in, in the age of enlightenment and at the beginning of the romantic era. He can no longer offer the girls incubi and thrills of fear.

Like all chroniclers of the diabolical, Goya did not believe in the devil and his works, but he was thrilled by the terror they aroused, and he used the terrible contact of fleshless bodies, gunshots piercing breasts, horns run through the belly, faces swollen with blows from fists; he showed bodies twisted with fear, crowds drawn together by the fascination of evil, in places of purification and exorcism. They are stronger themes than the banality of country life with which the princes were satisfied. Goya wanted draughts that burn the throat, rather than sweet drinks, and his career as a painter, engraver and designer is studded with scenes of murder. He desired them even before the war came and gave him so much real material. Is it not perhaps true that we appreciate life when near to death, and that reason is seen clearest on the borders of madness?

The orderly processions of peaceful festivals are replaced by assemblies full of screams and death-rattles, massacres, condemned men filing towards the scaffold, the sight of men garrotted or pilloried. Even at the level of daily life, at the level of "news in brief" or "legal proceedings" in the newspapers, Goya found images which have the same intensity as the Stations of the Cross. It is the same jeering, the same blood flowing from nose and mouth, the same acquiescence of the people, the same destruction of a fellow-creature by society. *Ecce Homo*, behold the man; only in Goya there are no faithful followers accompanying him to Calvary, because man is alone, crime has no remedy, and without a pause we begin again our conspiracies of death and rites of exorcism.

The dances were no longer the merry romps at San Antón, but lines of penitents swaying beneath the lash or twisting in their chains; masked balls now show the faces of madmen transformed into bears and fishes. The *Burial of the Sardine*, coming after *Blind Man's Buff*, is the blood-smeared burlesque in which the entertainment ends; the gay laugh has become a shriek.

Probably the writer who has expressed best of all Goya's passion at the gruesome carnival of humanity is the Belgian Michel de Ghelderode. The bonds between Flanders and Spain left scars on the spirit and chains on the flesh. His work *Hop Monsieur* ties in with the picture of the puppet thrown into the air by four girls, the Pelele of which Cervantes wrote in *Don Quixote*, and of which Goya painted an image full of bitter burlesque.

Goya was excessive in his representation of man and his acts. In his painting, other than portraiture, he no longer tried to show him in a state of happiness and order, but delved in search of the deep forces driving him, forces that could plunge man and society into a state of crisis. Goya never ceased to seek for the moments of liberation and truth. He looked for the reality of life in meetings in which everyone was face to face with fear, hope and hate. The clothes of the torero, the beggar or the carnival king, the chasuble and the pointed cap which the Inquisition forced upon their lost brothers, the crowns that madmen weave for themselves, all represent truths. Goya was no longer painting the conventional, reassuring pictures of popular life that the princes wanted in their palaces; they wanted peasants at their work and play; they wanted them shown poor as a reminder of the obligations of charity. But they did not suspect the power of the rituals of life or death in which the masses sought release or imposed their taboos. It was all inexplicable to the kings who remembered their French origins and made great efforts to lead the life typical of the rulers of the time. Perhaps they thought they could learn the truth about the people from the flamenco gatherings which provided folklore for foreigners. On the contrary, the truth of the people was to be found in carnivals and hospitals, in processions of flagellants, as it is today in stations, traffic jams, pop festivals, political demonstrations and at Lourdes. It was also to be found in the lunatic asylums. Few artists before Goya had set foot in asylums: Magnasco painted portraits of madmen, and Hogarth in the series *The Rake's Progress*, pictures the asylum to which the rake is reduced by his profligate behaviour. It is an asylum in which the madmen seem to be playing the part of madmen: they could be regarded simply as actors. In Goya the mad are confined in great vaulted halls with barred windows. Some individuals stand out from the dark melee, kings or popes who, under the rhythmic curve of the arches, abandon themselves to a multitude of incoherent gestures. The picture is the sum total of dynamic movements within a static composition. The prince with a plumed hat gives his hand to nobody to kiss, the pugilist fights against

nothing, the king talks to himself and the pope stands erect to bless the void. All are naked or almost so, all are covered with blood and sweat. No one had ever before depicted the disorder of the mind in such a direct way.

We can see the picture at the Academy of San Fernando at Madrid; beside it is a work which is probably not of the same period but which inspires the same emotion. It is a session of the Tribunal of the Inquisition—the terror. Torquemada had been sent to kill 8800 people. These tribunals were still functioning in Goya's time, but one of the first acts of King Charles IV had been to expel the Jesuits from Spain. The trials continued, but during his reign the only man condemned to death was absent, and only his effigy was burned. Goya thus saw the end of this system and showed it in its decline. There is no sensational confrontation in this trial, because they all seem depressed, sitting in front of a huge crowd following the debate, which is going on around four puppets in pointed caps. The Inquisition is no more than a machine which shudders and idles like the mad-men whose gestures are directed at nothing. Both the pictures show the same destruction of man in the role he has chosen or which has been imposed on him. The ill from which the lunatics

in the asylum and the members of the tribunal are suffereing is the same; it is a sickness of the spirit. In the first there are screams; in the second they are conversing in whispers, but the same feeling of emptiness prevails in both works. We find confirmation in another work, the *Procession of Flagellants.* Goya was attracted and repelled by the masses, by crowds of people, bodies pressed one against another, taking part in the same action and expecting to achieve something by it. In the *Burial of the Sardine* the festival has also something of the macabre in it. The burial of the sardine was a joyous festival which, on Ash Wednesday, meant the end of Carnival. Following a banner, a crowd in fancy dress carried a puppet to the bank of a river where it was burned. The rhythm of the dance shown was breathless, the dancers moving to-wards an anguish that transformed them. Goya bears witness to the ceremonies which Spanish society sought to keep alive and to promote values that were condemned and out-dated. Goya considered these tribunals, these dances, these processions as the ancient rules of a world in decline, that knew it could not last much longer.

Goya was perhaps without hope for humanity, sick and dizzy when faced with folly, cruelty and

fear. He certainly studied crowd behaviour and social life. The desperation of man stimulated the painter, and looking at his *Tribunal of the Inquisition* or at *The Madhouse*, we have to remember that Goya recognized Velasquez and Rembrandt as his precursors. The taste for chiaroscuro seen in the immense vaults beneath which the crowds assemble is surprising; it is the same taste as we find in the juvenilia of the Dutch painter. But it is an affinity of theme rather than style, because Goya knew Rembrant through etchings, not having had the opportunity to see his paintings. There is an affinity between the two artists, an equal attention to the appearance of things, their opacity and also their transparency. The last figures by Rembrandt, iridescent with colour, with a light slanting low as though in prayer, can be compared with a late picture by Goya, the *Milkmaid of Bordeaux*, in which all movement is replaced by the play of colour. But let us return to Goya at this dark, violent, dramatic stage in his work.

We have seen this style born in darkness, shot through by gleams of silver and electric blue. In the *Procession of the Flagellants* and the *Burial of the Sardine* the colour-tones are raised to the level of tumult. This was the moment when he published his first series of etchings, the *Caprichos*. The work, begun in 1793, consists of 80 pictures; it was put on the market in 1799 and withdrawn after two days. Despite this, 27 volumes were sold at a price of 320 reales each. In 1803 Goya gave the plates and the 240 remaining copies to the king. The reason for the gift was that he could not sell the book in Spain. The work was in demand abroad, but Goya preferred to give it to His Majesty rather than to keep it in the engraving studio, so that the fate of the work after the artist's death could be decided. We know the reason, an especially cogent one in countries strongly subject to censorship; official writers reproached some of their number with publishing abroad what could not be published in the country in question. Censorships are always patriotic.

Was this collection scurrilous? There were worse ones in circulation, especially books on the love of the queen and the favourite. But one of the king's painters could not play a part, however small, in a wave of satire on society and the properly constituted authorities. Goya realised this difficulty, as we can see from the very cautious announcement of his work which appeared in the Madrid press. He believed that painting, like poetry and oratory, could denounce error and vice, and that for this purpose ridicule was an efficient weapon. He added that this was an imaginative work, which meant that the satire was general and not directed at any one specific person. The work began with the artist's self-portrait, with a white cravat around his neck, his hair long and well-combed, his side-whiskers neat, his mouth disdainful, his eye deep, small, and coal-black. To crown it all, a tall hat. Goya depicted himself in profile, as an uncompromising, reserved, severe character, not handsome but powerful, a true denouncer of vice and error. This precaution, this guarantee was not enough. Historians describe the *Caprichos* as the work of a liberal denouncing an obsolete society, and consider the portrait in the frontis-piece to be that of a just man horrified by the dissoluteness of his nation. But this is not accurate; there is humour in the *Caprichos*, and there is humour in this portrait, which is too serious to be true, and hardly agrees with the fantasies that follow, or with Goya's other self-portraits which seem to contradict it.

Now let us look at these pictures with a different eye from that of the art-lovers who bought the book as soon as it was published. When a person is painted with the head of a cock or a donkey we cannot tell who it is meant to be, only that it is a vain or stupid man. Monks with ecstatic faces around a pulpit in which a parrot is declaiming means for us the adoration of an animal rather than a satire on preachers' inanities. Our time has accepted fantasy, which we interpret through psychoanalysis and not according to the rules of this bestiary. In the film by Bunuel and Dali *Le chien andalou* we find a sequence in which a man is seen dragging, with great effort, a piano bearing a donkey covered with blood, surrounded by rollicking poets. This sequence expresses the animal and the spiritual nature which the human being carries within himself. A *Capricho* by Goya shows two men carrying two donkeys on their shoulders; they are crushed by the stupidity of a world in which beasts of burden have become the riders.

We must add that the captions dictated by the artist have become, if not incomprehensible, at least difficult to interpret. In the *Caprichos* there are many obscure points which may baffle us, but anyway the work was meant to do that, and we cannot expect the artist to explain himself clearly because art should always leave a little ambiguity especially in satire. In many pictures the meaning is much more easily under-stood than, for example, in Hogarth's series on the life of a prostitute. For both the English and the Spanish artist, girls are always tempted by

4a. The Same Night,
Prado, Madrid

bawds who want to hand them over to rich lovers. Goya, who is less closely tied to a story, is clearer; with tears in his eyes he shows that sometimes these poor girls may be the victims of cruelty. One of them passes by a beggar woman without recognising her mother. There are also genre scenes like that of the girl who is being spanked for breaking a jug. There are "monkey tricks" as in Teniers, there is satire on old ladies who continue to adorn themselves to attract lovers, on drunken monks and deceiving women. They are all themes which we find in the books and engravings of the past. The tone is that of the proverbs which old men pass on to youths who do not listen: all that glitters is not gold, women are fickle, to trust is foolish, the doctors are asses, and so on.

In the *Caprichos*, this traditional criticism is combined with tragedy which appears in the first series of violent pictures. A woman abducted by two hooded men, a woman catching a last sight of her lover killed in a duel, women in prison, and a man carnally aroused by the corpse of a woman at the foot of a burial monument.

Witchcraft also plays a part in the *Caprichos*. The donkey is replaced by the he-goat; the old women who were used as a threat to naughty children carry them away in baskets and appear in a demonic group surrounded by sphinxes and bats. They journey into the anti-world, riding on their broomsticks, and become servants and adorers of a devilish people with pointed ears, hooves, claws and tails, who do not observe human laws, but mock the most sacred with burlesque professions of faith.

The *Caprichos* took between five and six years of work, and in the meantime Goya's style developed and his drawing changed. He is much freer in the etchings than in the paintings. Even while doing the professional portraits demanded of him, even while following his models with all the care they could expect, even while giving a very devout bearing to the saints in the church cupolas, Goya drew and etched the *Caprichos*, which means that he passed from a clear, simple, comprehensible expression of human reality and the celestial hierarchy to a complex study, often obscure, of the ill co-ordinated and scarcely understood part of the personality. He passed from the smooth, luminous, easily decipherable universe to a universe in which opposites meet, and where faith and reason have no certainty.

Thus the idea of Goya denouncing falsehood, vice and the anti-world, the image of the strict censor in the frontispiece of his collection, mouthpiece of the Spanish reformists, deaf, misanthropic and perhaps misogynic, are partial elements of a complex genius. The rejection of a false and distorted universe, full of monstrous laughter and ridiculous lamentations, in which

Sketch for Capricho no. 61
Volaverunt

society tries to correct morals and only succeeds in imprisoning poor girls, constitutes the unity of the book. A unity which does not exist outside Goya.

Everything from comedy to tragedy comes into this book; easy smiles and heavy witticisms, but also fear, and the fascination of a limbo thronged with monstrous beings, half man, half beast, places of execution in which young girls steal the teeth of hanged men by night, and cemeteries in which the dead lift up their tombstones. In this book we find Goya's fury against his times, a fury strengthened by the many demands on men; and this is the point which distinguishes Goya from the other caricaturists of his period. True caricaturists deal with topical events. Goya could indeed ridicule the girls of his time who take off their wigs and use them to sit on, but usually his etchings have more important themes; they insist that life is a sham, that dreams are peopled with monsters. Why live, then? It is an anguished, furious demand. To live is to wear a uniform that seems like a strait-jacket, to have your ears closed with padlocks, and to open your mouth only to swallow the potion doled out by a beast. Goya's etchings are protests against the purveyors of established truths, and against the way things were in Spain; they protest against fate and against conditions fixed by the divine will, but which man cannot accept.

Disasters of War
Por que.
British Museum, London

Ni par esas

Estragos de la guerra

Carretadas al cementerio,

Disasters of War
British Museum, London
Madre infeliz.

Y son fieras

Y no hai remedio

Las camas de la muerte,

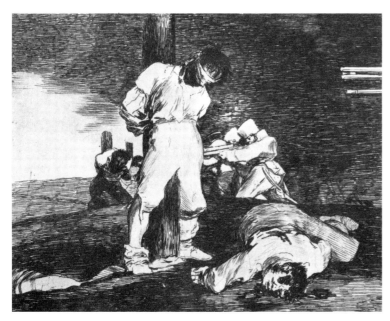

119

The etchings which Goya did after the lack of success of the first series, the *Disasters of War* and the *Disparates*, emphasise the same point with greater violence, because they have none of the humour of the *Caprichos*. Goya describes a world growing more and more vain and cruel, more and more absurd. Absurd but beautiful, even in wrongdoing, with white necks and magnificent complexions; exciting in the fights the outcome of which we eagerly await, amusing in the follies of the fat ladies, fleeing naked in the night, followed by their cat carrying a parasol, or going to a Sabbath on the arms of demons; or in the old men riding on each other to play picador against a wickerwork bull waved about by a rheumaticky friend; terrifying in the lecherous skeletons dear to Potocki.

If he had not enjoyed this beauty Goya would not have made so many etchings; he would not have returned—on the pretext of massacres, witches' sabbaths, bullfights and feminine wiles—to the same violent tension at the centre of the picture, the battle, full of shocks, soft sinuous movements and sharp points, to the nest of vipers, to the body that is flung down, wounded or dead. Though he would have liked to publish the *Disasters of War* and the *Disparates*, he did not succeed in doing so during his lifetime. His public work was that of an artist content with the outward appearance of the world, happy to paint kings, beautiful countesses and children in costume when he was asked to. His private work, on the other hand, said no to all women in beautiful clothes, all self-confident men in glittering uniforms. Goya found it quite natural to paint the portraits of Godoy, Wellington or King Joseph, and yet to study the horrors of slaughter in war, or circus tricks, or the panic of the crowd.

In all, 149 prints out of the original 228 of the *Disasters of War*, the *Disparates* and *Tauromaquia*, were carried out by intensive work between 1810 and 1820. In 1819 Goya signed the first lithograph made in Spain, the *Spinner*. In the great quantity of copper plates on which aquafortis, aquatint and drypoint were used alternately, there is not the same technical development as was noted in the *Caprichos*. It was rather the idea that was perfected: in the *Disparates* the black and white, the light and shade, are the very nature of the phantasms which Goya is depicting. From an admirable record he has moved on to a sublime creation.

The *Disasters of War* were born of the Napoleonic Wars; the desolation of his country was the confirmation of what Goya had foreseen

in the *Caprichos*, as he says himself on the first page of the collection. A man kneeling like Christ in the Garden of Olives has his arms spread wide before a black background on which can be read: "gloomy presentiments of what is about to happen". War is the moment of truth, when the worst part of human nature can be unleashed to kill, rob, rape and conquer. Stinking carrion—that is what men become. Damaged machines of death are repaired so that they can be sent to another massacre; and at the end bodies are flung naked into a ditch or cut into pieces and hung on trees because of a madness that shakes the earth before leaving it like a desert covered with flesh, a desert in which the stink of humanity speaks for itself. There was not another Goya to record the Second World War. But the same slaughter, the same hangings, the same armies of refugees, the same tortures, the same shootings began again. And today the same brutality still goes on.

Goya saw the heroism of the peasants in revolt and described it; he saw that the poor suffered in war more than the rich, and described it; his admiration brought him close to the people—that same people whom in peace-time he had judged with disgust as backward reactionaries. The war was for him a spectacle of violence. He painted scenes from the pitched battles between armies, in which he showed that brilliant strategist, General Palafox. He devoted his engraving to the images of personal courage or brutality. He could thus record the courage of the young girl of Saragossa who leapt on to the barricades to fire the cannon when the gunners were dead. Other engravings were inspired by the clash of small groups in which mortal fury is shown in all its power. He was not like the chroniclers of war who list the units involved, the captains directing the attack, the gunners aiming their cannon. He is concerned with that part where there are no names, and the soldiers are unknown, because for him war is not an art but a frenzy of murder.

The last pictures of the *Disasters of War* are metaphysical reflections; the events of which they treat are no longer the theft of sacred vessels, the rape of mothers, the looting of corpses; we are shown what human beings look like after the battle. The body is a covering of skin stretched over the skeleton. In Goya there are the same figures as we see in photos of concentration camps. For Goya this fleshlessness is the last stage before the corpses are piled up like mute masses shut in for ever in the centre of the page, in the centre of the earth, in the centre of

the memory. Waiting for the resurrection? So that his meaning may be clear, Goya shows a piece of human carrion under a whirlpool of figures, all laughing mockingly in the great storm that is dragging souls along, who manages with a great effort to write one word: *Nada*. Nothing: to die is to rot. The Life Beyond does not exist as people thought, that is, as the end of chaos, the place where everything will be bright. Death is neither the end nor a step from one life to another, but a slow disintegration, nothing more.

Then why bother to invent heresies or fight them, why worship and pray? Goya shows the great preachers as charlatans with parrots' heads, and Church dignitaries as rope-walkers. Life is a great beast that swallows and regurgitates men. Pilgrims are shown on a rope, tied to each other by the neck, groping their way like Bruegel's blind men.

Having seen the horror, Goya drew his conclusions. He had become more clear-sighted, putting aside all hypocrisy, continuing what he had begun in the *Caprichos:* the exploration of this shattering truth by which man is revealed through mobs in revolt and through violence. Princes and gods are only puppets passing temporarily over the slime of humanity.

Pessimism triumphs in this work of Goya's, even though there are a few flickers of hope here and there. There is in any case one element of certainty: the shining truth that scholars, bishops and monks cheerfully bury, but which flowers again, brighter still, despite all the blows they aim at it, and which can reveal itself to the most uneducated peasant. The uneducated perceive what the scholars miss: a young woman with a bare bosom and flowers in her hair. A shepherdess? The Goddess of Reason? These pictures show what Goya calls *la verdad*, the truth which is not Christ.

Was Goya an unbeliever, an atheist? In his Will, Goya wrote that he believed in "the Holy Trinity, Father, Son and Holy Ghost, three persons in one God, and in all the other mysteries and sacraments in which the Holy Mother Church, Catholic, Apostolic and Roman, believes". It was the prescribed formula, and children doubtless learned from their earliest infancy to make the sign of the Cross over all the letters they wrote. Ferdinand VII restored the Inquisition as soon as he came to power. Prudence was necessary; in any case some of his pictures show a passionate interest in the tragedy of Christ. Are the true Christians not those who suffer for the impiety of their times? It would be pointless to look for heresy in a series of engravings which denounce the vanity of all beliefs that separate men instead of uniting them. Goya did not reject religion, but he re-invented

it, away from philosophers, theologians, kings and soldiers. He loved truth because he loved Christ.

The word *capricho* authorised anything, so did the word *disparate*, but in the *Caprichos* there is elegance, a graceful comic side; the *Disparates* shows stupidity. According to modern dictionaries it means absurdity. The verb *disparatar* means to talk nonsense; the word *extravaganza* gives a good idea of the Spanish noun. It means wandering vaguely, seeing some things outwardly, some inwardly. The 22 pictures of the *Disparates* explore a rare, uncertain world, one that can be either inward or outward. The distinction is inexact because this is a study of humanity. Everything is bent, tortuous; the positions are crouching, the gestures are exaggerated, or the characters are enmeshed until they cannot move hand or foot. It has a ponderous reality, not at all spiritual, full of anxieties and unforeseeable shocks, swollen with unexpected growths, crushed by invisible powers.

Rembrandt 1606–1669—Dr. Faustus,
Petit Palais, Paris

These inchoate masses have nothing to do with our laws. Like Guardi in the same period, Goya too painted the ascent of a balloon carrying valiant aeronauts into the heavens. The victory over gravity seemed admirable to him, but in his engravings the victory had been achieved for some time. People flew on winged horses, on gigantic bats' wings or in an apparatus recalling the studies of Leonardo and the first aeroplane of Clement Ader. Bulls fall in clusters, in an endless shower.

Thus liberated, these beings find other places and become linked together in pairs, one weeping, the other laughing, one male, the other female. There is a woman with two heads, and groups made up of old men, young men, women and swordsmen, becoming one single entity, mingling cloaks and hats, entangled one with another, forming a sort of vague undulant presence.

The image of these human agglomerations gives a clearer idea of the spirit of the *Disparates*. Everything comes in: the scarecrow soldier, the dancer becoming gigantic, women abducted by horses, phantoms terrifying an army, the screams of masked figures. These elements, collected from every corner of the imagination are derived from children's stories. One day histor-

ians may tell us what deliciously terrifying Spanish grandmothers' tales Goya used. We can see that Goya also used fantasies that are common to all the legends in the world. He returns to certain themes already treated: the weakness of men in the face of women. The weaker sex, having sucked the life blood of the male, throws him into a sheet, or, witch that she is, emasculates and paralyses him; he also takes up again the theme of the rape of women. It is the struggle of the brutes, and the mass of masked beings obsessed with the idea of the graven image. The fairy tales that stimulated some of the *Disparates* give them a touch of the infinite, the detachment of human beings from earthly laws, their disproportion, their disharmony. Goya's strength was that he could create harmony from discord, without diminishing the force of his images. The *Disparates* combine all the obsessions of childhood which the adult never forgets, giving them a new force of expression.

The *Disparates*, like the *Disasters*, are full of references to Rembrandt. The two artists have in common the luminous quality of their work. Other similarities confirm that Goya was well

acquainted with the work of the Dutch painter. Rembrandt had painted Eastern wise men in meditation. Goya, on the other hand. shows them busy giving sacred texts to an elephant to read. Among the crowd he also shows Rembrandt's mother Neeltje bent over her stick, and Rembrandt himself laughing scornfully. In one of these crowd scenes we see a man with a turban and a naked sabre: it is Rembrandt again, rushing to save some Biblical hero, in this case Samson.

Such was the history of his images: an old woman posed for her son in Leyden, and then reappears in a bullfight in Madrid. She has lost none of her meaning, because she is still the same pious, affectionate old lady, now taking on a new role given to her by a different artist. An infinity of images, an avalanche of knowledge. The painter remains lucid, and draws from his subconscious what he puts into his work. The *Disparates* are made up of fundamental discords harmonised by the artist. The orderliness of composition overcome the madness of the themes and the disorder of the thought. Thus art journeys further away and annexes unexplored territories.

The *Disparates* have a parallel in painting: the black pictures which Goya painted in his country house on the other side of the Manzanares, the Quinta del Sordo, the deaf man's house. He painted them between 1819, the year he bought the house, and 1823, when he gave it to his grandson.

Detached from the walls on which they had been painted in oils, the pictures were exhibited in Paris at the Universal Exhibition of 1878, and then given to the Prado in 1881. The room containing these fourteen large pictures is a necessary part of a visit to the Museum, and the guide, indicating Saturn devouring a child, never fails to say that this picture was on the dining-room wall. The comment is the same in every language: how horrible. Why had the old painter decorated his house like that? Was he mad? The guide shakes his head and says he was peculiar.

Disasters of War: Sera lo mismo,
British Museum, London

Disasters of War: Asi sucedo,
British Museum, London

Disasters of War: Tampoco,
British Museum, London

Disasters of War: Amarga presencia,
British Museum, London

Scene at a Sabbath, sketch for the Quinta del Sordo,
Offentliche Museum, Basle

But certainly no more peculiar than in the *Caprichos*, the *Disasters* or the *Disparates*, or in some pictures like the *Colussus* which preceded this series. Painting is often considered as a pleasant ornament, and was thus accepted in the houses of all art-lovers, who were honoured to possess a Goya. In his house Goya was as free as he was in front of his paper or his copper plate. We find him in his natural state, like a king who need give an account to no one except God. With him are a child of six and its mother, the housekeeper Dona Leocadia. Goya is not in a boarding-house and he is not hiding away; neither does he want to decorate a hermitage for meditation. He is in his own house, and he is painting the drawing-room and the dining-room.

Are these nightmares? Goya was very interested in his dreams; he noted them, drew them, and covered the walls of the Quinta del Sordo with them. Only one picture remains mysterious, that of the dog buried in the sand, the most worn of all, the least attractive and the most disturb-ing. Elsewhere we find images referring to mythology or the Bible, like the Fates, Saturn, Judith and Holofernes, or to folklore like the processions to San Isidro or the scenes of the Sabbath.

"Cannibalism in the dining-room", says the tourist who has a still-life or an abstract picture in his own dining-room. Goya painted on the walls of his house scenes which we cannot say are dictated entirely by pessimism; he is a creator who knows the vanity of myths, actions and beings, and while continuing to paint them joyously and freely, asks himself the meaning of what he is doing, the meaning of art.

In this art we find the best of Goya's work. He can take an old theme—for example, that of the old gods of mythology and dead religions, or that of popular festivals, or that of the Deadly Sins and can create miracles of life, of living power. The dark side of life is as vivid, perhaps more vivid than the bright side. And Goya dedicated his house to it in mockery of the Prado.

Chapter V

GOYA AND RELIGION

The "capricious" aspect, in which the artist gives free rein to his imagination is the kernel of Goya's painting. A dazzling kernel, yet scarcely visible during his lifetime: the edition of the *Caprichos* was withdrawn, and the proofs of the *Disparates* were shut up in their folders while the artist lived. The black paintings were known only to a very few intimates though a few paintings, such as *The Madhouse*, were in circulation, Goya was known to his contemporaries as a portraitist, a historical painter, a church painter. Hence the persistent impression of his dualism as an artist—there were the official paintings and the private ones, the former belonging to the day, the latter to the night. In 1798 Goya painted his greatest public work, in which he expressed the great inward turmoil he preferred to all other themes—it was the decoration for the church of San Antón de la Florida. It is a bright caprice—if a dark caprice is what we call the paintings in the Quinta del Sordo.

The church had been built by an Italian architect: the painter's political friends were in power, and that made it easier for him to be given the commission. It was not a very important commission, because the church was remote, the nobility did not go there, the parishioners were probably humble people, and thus Goya had the field to himself.

The chapel was dedicated to St Anthony of Padua, and the theme could have depicted many miracles. Goya contented himself with one. In order to free his father, who was accused of a murder, the saint brought the victim to life before the judges; the victim then testified that the accused was not the murderer. That was all, and with that he proposed to decorate the whole

cupola. Under the arches supporting it he would put angels, and for the altarpiece an Adoration of the Trinity. In Padua many scenes of the life of St Anthony are told in the reliefs in the Cathedral. At Madrid, Goya confined himself to a single one in the clearest and most elementary way possible, so that he could paint what he had in mind—his own way of speaking to God and about God.

Next to the faithful, on the arches, he put seductive feminine angels holding theatrical curtains that rustle with wings or tulle; they are the flying support of the miracle we are about to witness. Looking at them, we guess that they are announcing a great spectacle: the saint coming down from heaven through the clouds, and with a solemn gesture raising the corpse amid the wonder of the crowd. Thus the sides of the cupola shine with spirituality. Goya had the example of Tiepolo, and the taste of the period was for these displays, which went beyond the boldest theatrical scenery. But this is different from either: the angels are close to us with their physical charms, the same as can be seen and admired in the streets every day. Goya's sky is

empty. It is a beautiful sky, crossed by clouds, in which the divine presence is not manifested by any special signs. The cupola becomes a stage, open to the sky. Goya has painted a railing of the sort which is usually placed outside windows for safety. Is it the balcony of a higher world? No it is the balcony that protects the crowds, an assembly of the people most typical of the painter's work, the fallen ones in the world below—our world. The angels are close to us; some look up at the sky, others look towards the faithful.

And St. Anthony? He is placed so that the servers at religious functions can see him. He is young and has a yellow halo. He is dressed as a monk, and bends over an already blackened corpse that is rising up towards him with folded hands. There is no tribunal, no old father grateful for the miracle, only the resurrection of a dead man. The congregation of the faithful, made up of customs officers and gardeners, asked no more. Having offered them what he was obliged to give them, Goya was free. His liberty was not such that he could paint anything that might offend the spiritual hierarchy of the church. We can emphasise that he painted real people as part of the cast of the miracle of St Anthony. He did not want to raise them to heaven, but simply to paint them.

At San Antón he painted as he wished, happy to be able to introduce his own world into the sanctuary of a church. The critics of this work have examined it in every way without finding anything in accordance with the usual way of representing the story. They therefore confined themselves to distinguishing the characters, about fifty of them, and picking out a few: the man running away, the man with a stick, the indifferent, the superstitious, the emotionally moved, the rich farmer, the visionary. All show the artist's indifference to the way the characters are dressed; some wear togas, others are dressed as peasants. There are women who seem to come from classical times, and others in the latest fashion, or with low-cut dresses worthy of Boucher. But it is not certain that Goya intentionally mixed past and present.

In fact the decoration of San Antón remains untranslatable in the theme, not because the artist was being deliberately obscure, but because he did not choose to order his thoughts on traditional lines. We can see in the foreground— the part with the angels—light movements, bright folds of curtain, and many scarves, winged women with plump smooth arms, a feeling of fluidity, the gleam of velvet. This unstable sweetness is a support for the terrestrial world, rough, aggressive, full of people in disharmony, but united in their humanity. Does it not perhaps mean that these living people, held up by the angels, are in a state of grace? Goya with his angels shows that the miracle happens within this human reality, and that in one movement the whole assembly enters a divine state. One gesture from a monk was enough to admit all this crowd to the state of grace.

For Goya the marvellous does not transfigure human beings. Some seem to be looking at the event, others are detached from it, or talking among themselves. The gestures of this crowd are not those of pilgrims; they have no religious meaning. They are the normal gestures that everyone makes. They are important because they give rhythm to a composition placed along the balustrade. They unfold a piece of white material on the parapet, harmonising it with the blue sky of the hemisphere. They give life to the lower part of the painting. The painter has put in all the characters from the human comedy, the whole of society, from the old man to the boy, from the hunchback to the girl, from the fool to the sage; he has put in all the gestures he loves and all the positions that his brush can render well. He has put into it his need to attribute a different presence to all beings. No one had been able to do this in a church before. But Goya's true liberty is in his technique; from a distance the work has none of the coldness which characterises frescoes, but feels warm, like an oil-painting.

Close to, certain figures have the dimensions of Romanesque frescoes, but not their conventional character. It is a riot of water, marble-dust, mortar and colours, with many unexpected novelties. To bring out the gold of a shawl Goya painted it with wide brush strokes which stand out from the woven material. The colour is, as it were, mixed in great waves, in separate touches so that from a distance it is unusually vibrant. Hence the sensation of colour not usually found in frescoes.

Goya would always have sought artistic liberty, because he was not disposed to treat themes in a conventional way. Frescoes had to be carried out rapidly, in nine or ten hours of work, while the plaster on the wall was still fresh. It was thus necessary to work quickly, and to improvise as far as possible. For that reason he refused to prepare the work, hence his argu-

ments with Francisco Bayeu on the scaffolding in the Church of the Pillar at Saragossa; his brother-in-law rebuked him for not following the sketch.

E. Lafuente Ferrari and Roman Stol, who have been able to study Goya's frescoes at close quarters, assure us that as early as 1771 Goya was painting with great brush-strokes. In his first and second attempts in 1780 in the same church, he was working as part of a team and so adapted himself to the usual formula with clouds, rays of light and all the pompous orchestration necessary on church vaults.

For the decoration of the church of Santa Cueva at Cadiz, which he decorated with three oil paintings, he had liberated himself from the tradition which imposed a certain accepted style of composition and interpretation of the subject. He painted his own reality, not that required by others, and thus showed us real human beings. To the faithful, this approach would not seem very orthodox. At any rate, we know works by Goya which leave us in no doubt of his religious feelings, and others which show his sentiments about priests. In religion as in everything else, Goya was against rigid formulas, but he used a church to make his views public by means of his art.

Chapter VI

AFTER THE KERNEL, THE SHELL

Hic jacet Franciscus a Goya et Lucientes hispaniensis peritissimus pictor magnaque sui nominis celebritate notus decurso probe lumine vitae obiit XVI Kalendas maii anno Domini MDCCCXXVIII aetatis suae LXXXV R.I.P.

This is the inscription on Goya's tomb at San Antón de la Florida. It is taken from his tomb in Bordeaux, where he died. Visitors flock to see it, but in the tomb there are two skeletons, one is that of Goya's mistress, Leocadia, the other is the painter's, but it is headless. The head is said to have been stolen by a Bordeaux phrenologist who wanted to study the bumps of a genius. Even after death, Goya's fate has a burlesque side, the same macabre aspect found in certain of his works. We might think at his tomb of his engraving in the *Disasters* in which the corpse rises to write *Nada*, or of the other in which we see a body cut into pieces as if on a butcher's slab. Certainly all is vain, all noble thoughts are false, spoilt by irrelevant accidents. Nothing happens in the straight clean way we are taught. These reflections are reinforced by Samuel Beckett's work *Happy Days* in which a woman (remember the dog in the Quinta del Sordo) is progressively buried. The first reaction of the audience is to regret the frivolity of this woman who is only interested in the brand of her toothbrush and what she has in her purse. Then the spectator is amazed by the intensity of her interest, and takes less notice of the poverty of the subjects; it is the liveliness of the interest that counts. Thus it is discovered that Winnie is still the centre of a miracle, life; and the subjects of her thoughts are unimportant; what matters is that she thinks, even in that state. While she is engaged in this exercise, however ill-applied and however ridiculous, hope survives, and in Winnie humanity continues to exist.

Beckett's lucidity and that of Goya are similar. Both seek life beyond the forms in which we perceive it. The words happiness and pleasure, anguish and despair are only ciphers, part of a code. Life can be interpreted in other ways, and Goya was one of the first to try to do it in a way that went beyond aesthetic novelty or variations in rhythm and colour, because the change came from the depths of his soul. Goya had imitators, but without founding a school, and thus he affirmed himself as a modern painter—the first one, that is, a painter critical of his own time, a painter seeking solitude; and his remoteness enriched rather than impoverishing him.

Meanwhile Goya was having a highly successful career as a Court painter, surrounded by the smiles of the most beautiful women of his time: those to whom he devoted the first stage of the decoration of San Antón, representing them as angels.

A glorious career, truly part of the period. The dates of portraits are always given, while in the works of imagination the date is left to the judgment of art historians, who tend to disagree with each other. The works which Goya painted for himself belong to a personal evolution and take their place in the artist's own interior sequence, whereas the portraits and official scenes fit into the time of kings and duchesses, and into the course of national history.

In 1795 he painted the portrait of the Duchess of Alba. He had just been appointed Court painter, the highest office for an artist, and he was 49 years old. Cayetana, thirteenth Duchess of Alba, was 33, and led a very unrestricted life. She had married at 13. In the first portrait of Cayetana and her husband, portraits which were intended to hang side by side, Goya paid more attention to the husband and his passion for Haydn's music than to the wife whom he showed as a large doll, imperious and abstracted, beside her dog. It is one of the most expressionless portraits he painted. The husband died the following year, and in the year in which she was wearing mourning, Goya painted another more vivid portrait (New York).

In this portrait, which never hung in the palace, but which Goya kept for himself, the Duchess wears two rings on her right hand, one with the name of Alba and the second with that of Goya, and she is pointing with her hand to the ground on which can be read in large letters the inscription (which had been covered with a layer of paint in a period in which X-rays could not have been foreseen), *Solo Goya*— "only Goya". It recalls those propitiatory actions with which lovers seek to confuse desire and reality.

There is a legend about the ardent love between the painter and the Duchess: it is said

that Goya had known her for a long time and that she influenced his work until her death in 1802. This means that any feminine figure might be the Duchess and that she might have represented Goya's ideal type of woman.

It is known that the artist accompanied the young widow during her official mourning in the castle of Sanlucar in Andulasia. From those days there remain two sketch books in the Madrid National Library and one at the Prado, one large and one small with pages missing. In these sketch books Goya noted down the ideas which he used later in the *Caprichos*. Between the scenes of monks playing tricks, sketches of gossiping society, scenes of dance and song, there are other sketches showing the life of a woman; she is combing her hair, stepping out of the bath, standing in her shift. They are intimate drawings; do they represent the Duchess in her private apartments? No one doubts that the drawings were done during the visit to Andalusia, and the missing pages lead us to believe that they have been censored. We know that the Duchess possessed a self-portrait of the painter and that she had given him a crystal goblet. There are two more engravings, one of which is called *Volaverunt*, showing a young woman in the sky, spreading her mantilla over three witches who seem to be providing her with rocket-propulsion. She is wearing the same

A Woman,
Bibliothèque Nationale, Madrid

A Woman,
Bibliothèque Nationale, Madrid

Ancient and Modern, sketch for Capricho 27,
Prado, Madrid

Sketch for Capricho 6,
Prado, Madrid

mourning clothes as the Duchess and has butterflies' wings. The second shows Goya trying to hold in his arms a double-faced woman surmounted with the same butterflies' wings. It is a dream-image, and the inscription confirms it: "dream of falsehood and inconstancy". In the *Caprichos* there are other allusions to an unhappy love-affair; the beautiful bird-woman whom the bird Goya is approaching, hooded and fluttering, is nothing but a trap into which every male must fall in the end. Everywhere a young *maja* appears, it is possible to call her the Duchess of Alba, but that is excessive; another error is to assert that the two *majas*, the nude and the clothed, are more or less portraits of her.

The New York picture proves the painter's respect for his noble model, and the passionate interest he had in her. It is for the novelists to decide whether this love came to anything, and if the association (always supposing it existed) lasted beyond the stay in Sanlucar, because we have no proof, and we cannot obtain any if it does not appear in private correspondence. Between the Duchess and her painter there was not a single letter, and no notes, not even those which she might have used to communicate with a deaf man. Nothing but drawings, which give us no certainty, apart from the picture where the two names, Alba and Goya, are associated. And is that not enough? We need to know more, as the painter did not express himself more clearly on this point. We must content ourselves with knowing that the son of the gilder of Saragossa had inspired, at least once, one of the most beautiful smiles in the Court of Spain.

Portrait of Dona Isabel Cobos de Porcel,
National Gallery, London, 1806

The Countess of Chinchon,
Sueva collection, Madrid, 1850

La Manola, Quinta del Sordo,
Prado, Madrid, 1819–1823

Portrait of the Countess of Carpio,
Louvre, Paris, about 1794–1795

Portrait of the Countess d'Altamira and her daughter,
Lehman Collection, New York, 1788

The story slips through the fingers, even though we can see the woman's eyes, her hands, her clothes, her hair—in fact her whole being, with overtones that words cannot express. In other portraits of women painted by Goya we see mother-of-pearl shoulders, slender hands, alluring gowns; it means that the painter's desire is ever new, and that every young model is challenging him to love her.

There are so many beautiful ladies before Goya's eyes: Dona Isabel Cobos de Porcel, the Countess of Chinchon, the Marquesa of Las Mercedes, the Countess of Carpio—to name but a few. Goya showed them with their jewels and their coiffures, giving each one all the force of her femininity. Goya loved to paint even those to whom nature had not been very generous: the *Woman in Grey* in the Louvre has rather fat arms, but what a rosy complexion, and how beautifully highlighted; and what skill in giving lightness to the figure by painting her in pale grey and pink in such a way that three vigorous brush strokes can reduce the impression of volume and highlight her very dark eyes and beautiful black hair.

The anecdote told by Goya in one of his letters, when the Duchess of Alba went to his studio and asked him to make her up, confirms the intimacy of relations between the painter and his clients, and the fact that they expected him to increase their beauty. The models had confidence in him, and to paint them he had to love them. The two pictures which could be hung one above the other with perhaps a particular impact, the *Clothed Maja* and the *Naked Maja*, prove that the painter, as he looked, was also free to imagine. There is a belief that insists that before an artist paints a woman's portrait he must know her intimately. It is said that Ingres prepared for the portrait of the Princess of Broglie by studying a young nude woman in the same pose as his model had chosen.

In Goya's case this reason is not enough; the Maja, nude or clothed, interests him above all as a sensual poem rather than as a study of a woman's anatomical proportions.

We must not forget that because of the Inquisition, nudes are rare in Spanish collections: the only glorious flesh that was tolerated was pierced with a spear, and even in Venetian decoration it was permitted only if it belonged to gods or goddesses. There was even a little Cupid included to make it clear that the beautiful woman painted by Velasquez was Venus. Even with the assurance that these delights belonged to another world, nudity was rare. In Spain, flesh had to be whipped, bloody, torn like that of Christ and the martyrs. Spain strenuously rejected the other promise of eternity offered by the flesh when it recalls, in a child, the presence of paradise before sin.

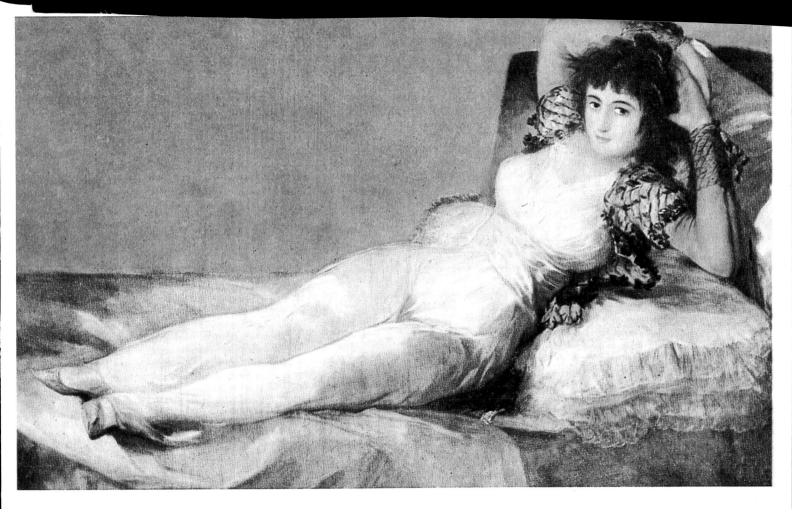

This rejection existed also in another form. Mythology had served this purpose for a long time. Erudition and knowledge have often been valuable means of concealment.

In the Prado catalogue we read *Naked Maja* and *Clothed Maja;* in old inventories she was called a Gipsy, while Goya's grandson insisted that she was the protegée of a gentleman, a girl without title, a beautiful woman without a name. In any case, the painting confirms better than words the truth about the artist and his model— he desired the figure swathed in pink silk, he wished to tear away the silk, to take off this second skin and gaze on all that sweetness. This gipsy which Goya painted, this *maja*—he did not intend her to be mythological, but part of the same world as his own, in which there were noblemen, actors, bullfighters and officials. Rather than a *maja*, she is the symbol of all the girls he had ever drawn or engraved. She holds the secrets of the most beautiful *marquesas* who posed for him, the promise of the *manolas* on the balcony, she is the earthly reflection of the angels of San Antón; she is Goya's ideal woman rather than a model. Goya personally did not look at women in the way shown in the *Caprichos*, in which the predominant theme is that of fickle woman and the fool who trusts her.

Clear and light, this nude recalls the naked back painted by Velasquez and reveals a new feeling. There is no desire to repeat the anatomical lesson of ancient statues, because the poet tells of the freshness of the complexion, the softness and fragility of the flesh. In the *Caprichos*, Goya's bitterness was applied to conventional themes. The two pictures under discussion proved that joy inspired him with a new, personal form. His eroticism makes of the

charming subject not a sleeping goddess as in Poussin, a fierce tigress as in Delacroix, a generous maidservant as in Coubert, a smiling libertine as in Boucher, but a woman for whom it is enough to exist because she is desired, a stillness stretched out in the light, a body in love-play with light. We are remote from the days of de Sade; we scarcely remember them.

For the court, Goya discharged the functions of Velasquez exactly; centuries may pass, but the service which princes demand of the painter remains the same: to paint their portraits and record history. But the same demands have given life to different creations. We must note that when Goya entered this environment there had been various attempts to break with convention. In Europe the portrait of a family or a group has had many variants. The Dutch had transformed it, with great humour, into a family excursion or a happy party at home. It is true that their clients were middle-class citizens. The Spanish remembered *Las Meninas* by Velasquez, a subtle work, with doors, arches, mirrors—the decoration for a scene of animation in contrast to the silence and stillness imposed by the stiffness of the composition. *Las Meninas* had not established a tradition, and with Louis Michel van Loo came portraits of the royal family in sumptuous and cheerful intimacy. The family was deployed in curves and counter-curves, in a setting with columns and tapestries, in a luxury in which the convolutions traced arabesques round the royal insignia lying on the table, dropped there like a burden that was too heavy.

Goya was the last to produce a masterpiece in this genre. After Goya, in the halls of the royal palace, there was only Winterhalter. We can consider Goya's portrait of Charles IV and his family as the last phase of an effort that had continued from generation to generation. It is a sign of the exhaustion of this artistic genre that the painter contented himself with simply lining up the subjects, without attempting virtuoso stage management. The same period in France saw the return of a style of painting which gave new life to the imperial portrait, which revived splendour, pomp and etiquette in Napoleon's time. Was it perhaps that the sovereign, to confirm his recent sovereignty, desired that it should be celebrated? Or because he wanted to see himself as Emperor? For the Bourbons in Spain, royalty was a habit, and there was no need to celebrate it; they did not need to be painted crowned, it was enough to be painted. The obsolescence of the genre and the subject led Goya not to revive official themes. Louis Michel van Loo had painted his sitters while they were talking amongst themselves, while Goya wanted silence, and put them in a line in an alternation of light and shade, as though clouds were passing between the group and the sun, or as though the hall of the palace had been opened and spring sunshine had come to light up the prisoners within.

Visitors marvel at this picture which they often consider an insult to royalty, and cannot believe that it was painted at Aranjuez in the sight of the Royal Family, and transported in 1814 to the Palace of Madrid; both Charles IV and Ferdinand VII were fond of it. Did the models not understand that they were being laughed at, and that they were ridiculous in their formal dress?

It is not certain that Goya was being satirical. It is true that some of the people look like puppets, and that it seems as though one need only cut a string and these travesties of men, stuffed with bran and covered with silk, would fall down. But this style, like shot-silk, brilliant and fascinating, was what was demanded in family portraits. It was not typical of Goya: this lightness, these men and women without

weight, made rather of silk gracefully pleated, are already to be found in Longhi. Goya saved it from affection by the subtlety of colour and light in a composition which gives the picture an intensely vibrant character.

Goya knew the royal family well; he painted the old king Charles III dressed as a huntsman not long before his death; he painted Charles IV when he came to the throne, and he painted the portrait of Queen Maria Luisa who loved clothes. He painted her in a crinoline dress which went back to the time of Velasquez. It is a marvel of tulle and ribbons. Looking at this picture we think of the sweetness of the angels in San Antón; the church decoration and the picture were done in the same year. Goya painted her on horseback like the equestrian portrait of the king, and he painted her with a plume in her hair, as a *maja* in a mantilla, and with one of those extraordinary hats invented by the milliners of the period. This fashionable lady stands with her elaborate coiffure next to the crown, which lies on an ermine rug. Which headgear does she prefer? The series of portraits of her is like a gallery of fancy dress which makes us smile at this woman of nearly fifty with a thin straight mouth and an imperious glare. This doll was the symbol of power in Spain. Her fancy-dress simply expressed in costume the confusion that reigned in Spain.

The worthy Charles IV only hoped to keep the peace and have a quiet reign. His wife was the breach through which disorder flooded in on him. He did not rule alone, because Maria Luisa had forced her lover, Godoy, on him as prime minister. Godoy thought he could play an important part in international politics, but he remained the leader of a Spain which was weak both as an ally and as an enemy. Goya also painted Godoy, but in a different spirit. The minister, who was at this time in command of the war against Portugal, is shown booted, before a captured enemy flag. He is admirable in this portrait, which is very close in style to French military portraits of the same period, a harmony of black and red. It shows the ease with which Goya passed from the silk of fashionable ladies to the leather of military generals.

Should we perhaps believe that because he could adapt himself to such diverse subjects, Goya in his capacity as Court painter was a traitor to himself? Has the real Goya disappeared? Goya observed everything in his period, but never with detachment, though sometimes from a distance. In the portrait of the royal family, Goya can be seen at work in the shadows.

A different type of lighting separates him from the royal family, which was said to live not in great intimacy but in strict dependence. The queen has at her side her two youngest children, said to be the children of Godoy: the young man in blue on the left was to plot against his father, becoming King Ferdinand VII. The boy next to him is Don Carlos, who later tried to overthrow the regent Maria Cristina. They are creatures united by the idea of power; they are together by virtue of the desire which was to lead them to fight each other. It represents the reduction of the conflicts of a country to a family level. The young woman turning her head away looks like a dressmaker's dummy and is a perfect illustration of the way in which the people in this picture are together and separate at the same time. She is in fact hardly sketched in; the Infante Ferdinand was not yet married and Goya was reserving the place for his future wife by showing an unknown girl. History tells us that her name was Maria Antoinetta, and that she came from Naples two years later.

Queen Maria Luisa with a big hat,
Prado, Madrid, about 1789

Portrait of Don Carlos Maria Isidro,
Prado, Madrid, about 1800

Portrait of Dona Maria Josefa,
Prado, Madrid

Why did Goya not finish the painting? Perhaps because the picture went to the Royal Palace and the queen detested her daughter-in-law. For us it is a chance to see how Goya invented a character. He imagined her young, and put her in full light like a beautiful fleshy fruit, with a more sensual appearance than the wife of the Prince of Parma on the right. A young woman, for him, had this rounded breast and long neck, and as he could invent her dress, he bathed the silk in a golden light that no woven material could ever give.

At the Prado there are five preliminary studies which help us to see how Goya worked. Whereas Mengs painted on a cold, neutral ground, Goya painted on a warm ground, an all-over ochre, which he covered with brushstrokes in white, pink and red. The delicate white is sometimes toned down but often shines in all its splendour. The brown, transparent over the ochre, becomes like velvet. It is a most subtle art, admirable in its poetic fancy. Every brushstroke is a transfiguration, every colour exists not in itself, but always in respect of another colour, in a sort of transparency, bound to a common base; the ochre of the background warms the other cold colours. In the sketch for the portrait of Maria Josefa, the old lady with the black spot on her temple, Goya is debating with himself: the painter who was accustomed to portraits and knew their subjects and their technique, hesitated when faced with the black spot. He had never had occasion to paint one, and he tries a colour at the bottom, on the neck. It works, and so he can paint even a melanoma.

Portrait of Gumersinda de Goya,
Noailles Collection, Paris, 1805

The use of transparence and impasto gives the idea of silk, of faces, of hair, of hands, and behind the brilliant, empty figures whose mediocrity is wearisome to the eyes, there is this prodigious feast of colour. Such is the dualism of a work of art. To give an idea of royalty and its pomp, Goya had to set up a tremendous feast of colour and rhythm. During the sittings, the models had taken an affable, benevolent attitude; in the picture Goya preferred a tense expression, almost adding anxiety to their faces. For the decadent nobility of the principals he substituted another nobility, another strength— his own. In the picture, the king, the queen, their heirs and relatives, are only putting their heads into the web of light and shade, of alternating and changing colours. The painter is a little apart, in the shadows but on a level with the king, on the same plane. At a recent restoration, it was discovered that this area of the painting was not as empty as was thought; there is a picture of a naked man attacking two semi-naked women. This is in the gilded cornice on the left, while on the right is a very stylised landscape. The picture is the same type as the bacchanals of Rubens or Jordaens with the Goya touch in addition. It is thought that the man on the left is Goya, and that the painter wished thus to introduce real passion behind the noble and calm appearance of the models. It has also been said that the artist's intentions were moralistic, and that he had dared to denounce the falsity of this apparently noble family reunion. Anything is possible, even though this second interpretation is scarcely probable. What can be said of the shadow which the painter placed in front of the figure of the future King Ferdinand VII? Did he foresee the dark years which Europe was to pass through under the rule of this prince?

Goya was neither a visionary nor a magician, and I would rather think of him as simply a painter. He needed to enliven the dark parts of his painting and create movements of light, the only movements possible in this static composition. As for his resemblance to the bold lover, it ought perhaps to be attributed to the law by which artists have often painted self-portraits (this happens also in Rembrandt) and to their habit, often involuntary, of depicting themselves everywhere. There is no need to consider this picture as a satire, because Goya painted his models as he saw them and as he thought of them; not as unreal, because realism is not what one sees but what one knows, and Goya knew.

The man in the shadows painting the royal family achieved success. The publication of the *Caprichos* was suspended, but Goya, with this royal commission, attained a position of the first rank, and to be the choice of King Charles IV was flattering. From his youth the king had acquired works by Raphael, Ribera, the Master of Flemalle, Andrea del Sarto—artists with different styles. Until 1817, though with varying fortunes, the painter's life was associated with the life of the royal palace. As court painter he earned 50,000 reales a year, he had his lodging free and was given 500 ducats for the upkeep of his carriage. In addition he painted many portraits of the nobility of Madrid, and for every portrait he earned from 5000 to 8000 reales.

His lodging was comfortable, as can be seen from the inventory made after his death; there was a bronze clock adorned with two cherubs, a white and gilt table, Louis XV chairs ornamented in silver, and carpets. The interior decoration was white and gold, as was fashionable at the time. The pictures on the walls were dark but vivid and tasteful in their controlled intensity. There was a Ribera: *St Peter*, an El Greco: *Virgin in Meditation*—works by Coreggio, Tiepolo and Velasquez, besides the painter's own pictures including a portrait of

the king, a self-portrait and the portraits of his family: his mother Gracia, his wife Josefa, his son Javier and his daughter-in-law Gumersinda. The two young people were married in 1805 when Javier was 21. His father painted him fashionably dressed, with a cane in his hand, a black two-cornered hat, light shoes, striped trousers and a grey jacket, a pleated shirt; a little white dog lay at the feet of the young man, who later had the title of Marquis de l'Espinar. Gumersinda is shown wearing a magnificent lace veil and gloves reaching past her elbows, and beside her is a white dog like those owned by great ladies such as the Duchess of Alba. Goya, on the other hand, liked to show himself unadorned, with an open neck and unkempt hair, thus accentuating the contrast between the two generations.

In the first years of the century Goya's position was enviable; his work did not keep him very busy. His neighbours were famous artists: La Tirana, Isidro Maiquez, and the bravest toreros like Pedro Romano, the master of Ronda. Goya painted their portraits. He was also surrounded by many intellectuals, Bernard de Yriante, a patron of the Academy of San Fernando, the playwright L. F. de Moratin, the poet Melendez Valdés, the diplomat Urquijo, the economist Jovellanos. Though he associated with Godoy in his capacity as official painter, Goya had friends belonging to the opposition who were trying to seize power. Jovellanos was Minister of Justice and Urquijo Secretary of State. Their careers were beset by difficulties; they were persecuted by the Inquisition, arrested and tried for giving a character in a play too natural a speech, for translating Voltaire, for writing the introduction to a translation of Rousseau. The life of these men alternated between important offices—in which they thought that they were in command—and

prison. That seems to be the rule in times of intense political struggle when democratic laws are not applied. Laws did not function in Spain, a backward country in which the government was in continual disagreement and thus could not bring about better conditions. The weight of tradition was such that the new ferment in Europe had filtered through to only a small section of society. War, moreover, was at the door, and the armed forces could not smooth out so complex a situation; they only aggravated it. The liberal party favoured by Goya considered the clamours of the French Revolution as the beginning of new hope for their own country. Nobody wanted the abolition of the monarchy—they simply wanted reforms, a less mediocre government, and greater freedom. Foreign powers took no heed of these aspirations; England, for example, saw in Spain's weakness the possibility of expanding her own colonial territories, while Napoleon's France needed Spain to weaken the English blockade. Charles IV and Ferdinand VII were not good risks, and Napoleon sent in their place his brother Joseph Bonaparte, who arrived with a liberal programme and at once won the support of the Spanish intellectuals. Melendez Valdés was the new king's adviser, while Moratin became Director of Libraries. Their need for freedom attracted them to the side of the French. The majority of the population, forgetting that the sovereigns of their country had always been of foreign origin—Hapsburg or Bourbon—resented the intrusion and fought against the new king's troops, and in the liberal camp there was great confusion, which did not prevent them from obtaining a sort of Constitution from Ferdinand VII. Of Goya's five friends of whom we now have records, only one, Jovellanos, died in Spain. The others, like Goya himself, died in exile in France.

We may wonder whether Goya, in choosing these friends, was choosing liberalism or the company of the liveliest intellects of the period in Spain. Goya was accustomed to court life, and was very shrewd. The captions to the *Caprichos* are a combination of daring and prudence, provocation and morality. He belonged to a generation which was practised in the contraband of ideas. His deafness was a means of defence, because how were people to behave with a man with whom you had to communicate in writing, who talked in monologues, and whose only real means of expression was in painting? As an official painter he did what was asked of him, and in his engraving he applied the rule: "Render unto Caesar the things that are Caesar's".

For many years Caesar was uncertain, unstable, ephemeral, and events brought Goya a redoubled influx of commissions. Scarcely a king came to power, scarcely an important personage entered Madrid, but the court painter had to paint his portrait, as though the portrait were a confirmation of his investiture.

There was open war between Charles IV and his eldest son Ferdinand VII. A first attempt to seize power ended with the young claimant to the throne being imprisoned. It was the moment at which French troops were entering Spain in order to fight and conquer Portugal. The second attempt led to the abdication of Charles IV. Ferdinand VII was king, but he returned the crown to his father, who in his turn offered it to Napoleon. Joseph Bonaparte was proclaimed king of Spain. Goya painted them all, except Napoleon. In May and June he painted the equestrian figure of Ferdinand VII for the Academy of San Fernando, a large picture in which the king is holding in his hand a stick surmounted by a crown. It is a fine work in which the painter does not forget a single decora-

tion or ribbon which would emphasise Ferdinand's royal office. The hat is enormous, the coat is grey under a blue and rose sky, and the figure is placed at the point of intersection of two diagonals which give a stiff, severe effect to the composition.

The following June, the country had one king but two Councils, one at Madrid supporting Joseph, and the other at Aranjuez supporting Ferdinand. Thus nothing was changed except the king. Everything was ready for war; all that was needed was the signal, which was given by the clash between the people of Madrid and Murat's soldiers. Spain became a great battlefield for the respective ambitions of Napoleon and Wellington. Liberals and reactionaries, monks and anticlericals, aristocrats of various parties, all flung themselves into the melée.

Goya engraved and painted, and also attended the sessions of the Academy. King Joseph had changed nothing in the organisation of the arts, except that Godoy's palace had been turned into a museum in which were housed the royal pictures and the immense collections built up by the monasteries, which had been confiscated. With the same decree, Joseph had ordained that 50 pictures should be given to his brother Napoleon to serve as an example of the Spanish school in the Musée Napoléon. A Commission was appointed, and Goya was one of its members. The Commission was not very diligent, and took more than two years to draw up a list. The selected pictures were placed under strict security, at least so it was thought; in fact seven were stolen and had to be replaced. In September 1813 the pictures had not yet gone, but finally they left Spain to the accompaniment of a certain furore. It was said that the Academicians had had time to make copies, trusting that the French delegates would not notice. Copies of the works sent to the Musée Napoléon were

returned to the Prado, and figure there under the names of the presumed authors: they are works by Velasquez, Ribera, Navarrete, Zurbaran, Cano, Bermejo, Pereda, Collantes, the elder Herrera, Morales, Murillo and Ribalta. The inclusion of the elder Herrera, the rough master of Velasquez, reveals the taste of the period, as does also that of Bermejo.

In relation to plans for creating a Museum in 1809, the year of the decree, the city of Madrid declared that it wanted a portrait of the new king in the decorations of the Ayuntamiento. Unable to get Joseph to pose, Goya created an allegory in which the city of Madrid is shown as a young woman holding the coat of arms in her right hand and pointing with her left hand to a medallion carried by angels and surmounted by Fame blowing a trumpet, while Goya carries a crown of laurel. In the medallion was the new king's portrait. The work was painted in a little over two months and hung in the hall of honour. In August 1812 Joseph left Spain on the arrival of the English army. The city fathers realised that they could not greet Wellington with this tribute to the usurping king. The portrait of the king was covered with a layer of paint on which was written the word Constitution; this showed that even after Joseph's departure the liberals wished to maintain the rights he had instituted. In November of the same year the fortunes of the armies changed and Joseph returned. His portrait had to reappear. Goya sent an assistant who took off the paint and the word Constitution and brought back Joseph's face. Cost, 80 reales. In May 1813 came a new alarm; Joseph fled a second time and Goya had the word Constitution re-painted at a cost of 60 reales. With the succeeding political changes, the same medallion received, as necessity dictated, the portrait of Ferdinand VII or the phrase "Book of the Constitution". At last, in 1872, came the final version with the words *Dos de Mayo*. That is how history, with its words of command and its dictates, influenced Goya's painting. Here is another example.

When Wellington entered Madrid in 1812 it was not enough to wipe out Joseph's portrait; the conqueror's portrait had to be painted. In twenty days Goya delivered a large picture. Chroniclers tell us that the painter was nervous, partly because of his wife's death. The British Museum has the preliminary sketch, and the Wellington Museum the large canvas, in which the Duke is executing a caracol on horseback, dressed in black with a red belt. It is a fine picture. At 66 Goya was still a virtuoso; only recently has it been discovered how he managed to complete the portrait so quickly. Radiography has revealed that it was originally conceived as an equestrian portrait of Joseph so that when Wellington arrived all Goya had to do was change the head, and produce an Englishman instead of a Frenchman.

What was Goya's opinion in the conflict? The artist painted portraits of many members of the government, of the usurper king, and even a French general; as a friend of the liberals he followed those who helped King Joseph. But even so we cannot believe that Goya was interested in politics. In his work we find agreement with both the right and the left, because as a painter Goya was always in control of appearances. Remember the fury expressed in the *Disparates* and the *Disasters of War:* the truth was not in the warring parties but above them. From the depths of his mysterious inner world Goya saw men arrive and depart, almost as the director of a Seismological Institute registers earth tremors. How can a witness be asked to select his subjects? Goya had seen war and men at war, and did not divide the good from the evil murderers, the guilty victims from the innocent.

No one expected him to take up a stand. Joseph kept Charles IV's portraitist in his job, and Ferdinand VII made no change. He had been asked to paint Madrid's homage to the usurper, the revolt of the people of Madrid against the Mamelukes, and the shooting of the hostages by the French troops. Beethoven was Kapellmeister to Jerome, King of Westphalia, yet he composed the Battle Symphony in honour of the Duke of Wellington.

Goya set to work in 1814, six years after these events, and painted the portrait of Ferdinand VII in royal robes. He also showed General Palafox, the hero of Saragossa, in action, riding towards the gunfire and shouting orders. Goya thus proves his epic power. He also painted two large pictures, *The Second of May* and *The Third of May*.

Legend has it that Goya was present at the two brutal scenes, field-glasses in one hand, pencil in the other, and a gun by his side. Whether Goya was present or not is unimportant. It is more important to notice that the painter has brought on to the stage a new protagonist—the people, that same people who were to appear in the great compositions of the 19th century.

Costume historians who have studied these pictures have noted that apart from the crimson, purple or scarlet trousers, the Mamelukes' dress is not accurate. At the execution, the bayonets, the shakos and the green capes are the only elements which allow us to suppose that the firing-squad is composed of soldiers from the Corps des Chasseurs. He was not trying to satisfy the experts on the uniforms of the Imperial armies: as a military painter he could record all the details of the uniforms and decorations of Godoy or Ferdinand VII on the battlefield. In this case, however, he was recording a

169

battle of unknowns, without rank; men different in race, language and dress.

In the first picture, *The Second of May*, there is a surge of horses and men, a host brandishing weapons, and we see the reality of battle, with murder close at hand. It is not the usual ballet of war that appears, for example, in the engraving by the Frenchman Adam, *The Capture of Saragossa by Napoleon's Troops*. There they are all threatening each other with expansive gestures, but there are few corpses, and we do not see men dying. They fight or they are dead, as in a children's game of war. No one is dying or bloody. In Goya, blood spurts; it smears the face of the man sinking his knife into the horse's flank, or flows on to the fallen Mameluke. The work is a seething mass of men stabbing each other; it is death in action in a group. The feeling of mass is given especially by the horses pressed against each other, rather than by the crowd in the background who are fighting with sticks and daggers. The essence of this mass movement is contained in a triangle formed by three men looking towards the centre: the man dressed in green who is stabbing a white horse, the Mameluke brandishing a dagger, and the hatted *majo* who is stabbing a Mameluke in the belly with his own dagger. The visual field of the three men is also the field of action of the three armies battling face to face. For Goya it is a question of war man to man, and there is nothing in his composition that could interest a strategist or disgust a general.

The second picture, *The Third of May*, is even more important because of the opposition between those who are shooting and those who are being shot at. The former emerge from the shadows like a machine for killing, rooted in the earth amid a complex play of menacing shadows. It is a succession of tragic moments: prayer and fear, the shock of death (a white ray

of light on the shirt of the dead man with outstretched arm) and the transformation into bleeding flesh. From this image, with a subtle interplay of material and colour, a work of art is derived. The firing-squad is painted in very thick colours, which gives them a dark and solid appearance. On the first soldier's arm there is a metallic patch of moonlight. The victims, on the other hand, are treated with exceptional delicacy of colour, opaque and transparent by turns. The riot of colour is for those who are dead or about to die, and if we can bear the sight, we should look at the corpse in the foreground; the blood does not obscure his features, but brings them out in all their beauty.

War had never been shown like this before. In the primitives, in the manuscript painters, in Bruegel and in Callot, we find massacres of virgins, the beheading and torture of Christian mystics, the occupation of cities, with the inhabitants put to the sword. We also find a little violence in Gros's picture *Napoleon visiting the plague-stricken at Jaffa*, painted a few years earlier, but there was something exotic in it. Desperation did not go as far as the panic-stricken expression of the horses, and the wild eyes of the combatants did not touch the glittering reality of murder in a city square gilded with mild Spring sunshine. No one, moreover, had ever painted the precise moment of revolt. Dürer had made plans for a monument to the peasant's revolt: at the apex there was to be a peasant with a sword buried in his back. The revolt had been put down, and the monument was a funeral one. In Goya the crowd is dynamic, and shows that it can defeat the best of troops. Napoleon's Mamelukes numbered no more than 120, but they were known throughout Europe.

In the shooting scene, the crowd has become

passive and is letting itself be massacred. Yet the monument which Goya raised to this martyrdom is still a reminder of the strength of the crowd on the previous day. Ferdinand VII, when considering his future as a king, must have taken into account the existence of this populace, which the painter had brought into the royal palace. The two pictures were soon moved into the Museum, where they were not safe from the hazards of war: during the Civil War a lorry transporting *The Second of May* from Valencia to Catalonia had an accident and the canvas was torn. The lacerations can still be seen on the left side, because it was not repainted; a neutral colour similar to Goya's ochre background was applied.

Goya had succeeded in making heard the voice of the crowd, the same voice as resounded in the vault of the church of San Antón de la Florida, the same true human reality, not the isolated individual being but the collective being, the being in society, the human race.

How very different this is from the crowd he painted between 1815 and 1818 in what was known as *The Assembly of the Philippines* (Castres Museum). It is his largest picture, the same size as Rembrandt's *Night Watch*, and to understand two nations as different as the Dutch and the Spanish, two societies as different as a republic and a monarchy, we ought one day to exhibit the two canvases side by side. The history of this Assembly is not well documented, but we can identify some of the people. In the centre of the platform is Ferdinand VII and the President, Munarris, whose portrait Goya painted. A meeting of governors is being held to decide the economic and political future of the Spanish possessions in the Philippines. The picture is a wide open space in which the people are arranged or rather submerged; it is Goya's reply to *Las Meninas* of Velasquez. *Las Meninas* was a painting in which silence reigned among the leading actors in a theatrical setting. *The Philippines* is also the setting of a work in which the leading actors are missing and only the supporting cast is there.

The work is noteworthy from two points of view. The king is presiding, but his chairmanship is accomplishing nothing. No assembly gives the idea of intense activity, but no one had ever shown quite such a sleepy board of directors. The painter has shown us men in a state of prostration. The second point is that faced with such decrepitude the painter was able to impose his own will and do as he liked with this subject, the fate of the Philippines having become of scant importance. There is a king in this theatrical work, and Goya placed him in the centre. But the real king of the picture is the sun. Goya arranged the figures in a pattern of vertical, horizontal and diagonal lines, showing their gestures, their positions, their clothes, while some are looking at the floor and others at the ceiling. The real object of the session is silence, not the future of the islands. The real subject of the picture is light, which falls in a colourful stippled effect. Unity returns in the representation of the curtains, the faces, the legs crossed in front of the chairs. The picture recalls David (*The Coronation of Napoleon*, 1805–1807, was painted not much earlier). David had a habit of weaving his figures into the pattern of the painting, especially the background figures. Those in the foreground had to be shown as the important personages they were.

Goya was seventy when he painted this picture. *The Assembly* is one of the artist's boldest creations; he was tackling, in immobility, themes which he had treated in agitated compositions and extremely lively rhythms. No baroque artifice could have emphasised this motionless torment. Two pairs of eyes be-longing to the two people sitting at either side of the picture at the same level are raised to the ceiling and form a sort of isosceles triangle which is superimposed on the rectangular shape of the whole composition. Above the rows of figures along the walls a greenish mist circulates through which the ochre of the background shows in places. The mist rises from the large window on the right, and thus a luminosity is born. The light carries on a dialogue with the subject, and overwhelms it.

Goya's public work is concluded with this severe message proclaiming the dominance of the void. It is the last phase of an official career which had developed to an extraordinary degree. In this picture Goya, even though submitting and adapting himself to the situation and the commission, still gave free rein to his thoughts. The great emptiness of the picture is the emptiness of Spain, and after this emptiness he was to paint the walls of the Quinta del Sordo. In the struggle between the fullness of his imagination and the emptiness of his country, it was emptiness that won. In 1823 Goya gave the house he had branded, in which he had painted the proofs of his imaginary journeys to another world, to his grandson Mariano. The latter was 17 years old, and we can imagine the effect it must have had on this boy to take possession of such a place. It has been said that the gift was made in the fear that the artist's goods might be expropriated. In that same year Ferdinand VII had called on the French army to re-establish absolute monarchy, which he had had to give up on conceding the Constitution. With war at the gates, the painter asked himself whether he was likely to come through this trial as he had through the earlier ones; and, being in doubt, he had to save his own property. As for his independence, he had that, even if the government ordered no more portraits; but Ferdinand,

like Joseph, wished to create a public museum. When the Prado opened in 1819 Goya was there with two portraits, of Charles IV and Maria Luisa.

We should perhaps see in this gesture the final renunciation of a man who had had everything and did not care to die in his house like a king in his palace. Madrid, moreover, had no longer any importance for him, his post of court painter having become a meaningless sinecure. Goya preferred to depart rather than to stay and wait for commissions that did not come. Many of his friends had fled to France, and in 1824 Goya too decided to leave, at the age of 78. His pretext was that he wanted to take the waters at Plombières, but in reality he lived in Paris and Bordeaux, and thus the artist who had always lived in Spain became a traveller.

He spent the last years of his life travelling between Bordeaux and Madrid, where he was always well received. In 1826 he had his portrait painted by Vicente Lopez and resigned from a post he no longer occupied. Goya returned to Bordeaux where his housekeeper Leocadia awaited him with her two children Rosario and Guillermo.

There were political and emotional reasons for the painter's going abroad, but not enough to snatch away an old man from his son and grandson whom he loved. Was it impossible to go on living in Madrid, reconciling his affection for his son with his affection for Leocadia with whom he lived? As a court painter he would have been able to go on painting official portraits if they were commissioned. Could the artist who had captured the fascination of the Spanish crowds in war and at the *corrida* have forgotten the life of the Spanish street? Probably the artist went away to escape from daily routine, fixed timetables, and the regularity that usually prevents us from seeing that we are travelling towards death with gathering speed; and besides, he needed change and movement. In going away, Goya left his works, the glory attached to his name in churches and palaces, and he abandoned the people he knew. He left behind him everything he had done in 70 years of work, to move to a country in which he was almost unknown.

In Paris and in Bordeaux where he settled, he continued to paint and engrave. He did lithographs for the printer Goulon, but he could not think of starting again on a new career. His rate of production had slowed down; he painted only small canvases and miniatures on ivory. He lived within his means and associated only with Spaniards, many of whom had chosen to live in Bordeaux. The historians speak of daily meetings at the shop of a chocolate-maker from Saragossa where chocolate in white cups was set before the great man who was seated in his special armchair. These are trifling landmarks in a life that began at Fuendetodos and ended in Bordeaux, where the painter, having been deaf for more than thirty years, may have felt no more a stranger than at home, but with fewer ties.

Some prefer to die in their own home, surrounded by their family, among the reminders of an active life. Others prefer to leave everything, to become as naked as when they were born, and to end life lightly, as though they had been able to free themselves from every chain. Goya did not want to break with everything, forget everything, let go the moorings. A few days before he died, his grandson Mariano came to see him, and Goya gave him a letter for his son Javier: "so much joy has upset me that I have had to go to bed." It may also be that Goya wanted to go to France so as to be no longer the court painter but a simple man awaiting the end. In *The Assembly of the Philippines*, the scene was presided over by a void; the artist's spirit entered this void on April 16th, 1828, at two in the morning.

pez a su Amigo Goya

Chapter VII

BOBALICON

One of Goya's last works is a woman in profile, *The Milkmaid of Bordeaux* (1827). The contours are not precisely indicated, and the hands are only hinted at. The artist has not sought the values which usually interest art-lovers, that is to say those who ask for a portrait of their wife in a beautiful dress with ribbons tied at her waist. The general lines of the picture are very simple: the woman is in the centre, at the point of intersection of the two diagonals. It is a young face, an unusual beauty which would have interested a Venetian painter like Titian or Veronese. The model's features interested Goya less than the opportunity she gave him to study light yet again. The young girl is wearing a blue-green bodice with a little white shawl on top of it, crossed over in front, and a kerchief on her hair. What do we see in the picture? A little figure which the light models, on which it falls in patches, and the patches are more important than the shawl they outline or the breast they model. The luminosity is like foam spreading over a shape, breaking it up and recomposing it. The little shawl passes through a spray of clear blue light and green shadows. No one knew that a milkmaid could evoke the depths of the sea, rain-forests and the rose-colour of flowers or flesh, simply because she was seated with the sun shining straight down on her. Goya shows us how; and Impressionism is born in this work. Did Goya perhaps foresee an art in which colour was transfigured by light, which becomes the real subject of the picture?

Goya went back to Rembrandt who in his last paintings had reached a stage in which art does not gesticulate; he does not wish to re-invent expressive forms, but finds all his splendour in the interplay of colours. Rembrandt lit the mysterious fires of colour in portraying contemplative beings, closed in on themselves, rapt in that immobility that precedes the end.

We have tried to show in his work both the imaginative and the official side, and we have noted that the phases of creation met many difficulties, and that the official aspect of the painter was as revealing as the private side. In this way we have found Goya's unity in his painting.

Goya was a master of drawing, as his engravings reveal, but for him black and white were colours. Sometimes he chose a certain line because with it he could weave lace, give a serpentine movement to embroidery, or caress the curve of a *Maja's* hips. But his real drawing was a work of light in a field of shadow, black clouds drifting across a clear sky. His pictures always have weight, colour and ruggedness. For Goya, art was to work on the material with pencil, charcoal and paint, and to make it express pain or joy. Between him and the plaster of the frescoes, between him and the colours mixed in thick masses on the palette, there was terrific tension.

When we see him paint the study for the figure of old Maria Josefa in the portrait of the royal family, we note the skill with which he makes the colours sing in their airy flow over an ochre background, and achieves a velvet effect in the meeting of two brush-strokes. But when he painted the vault of San Antón de la Florida using his fingers, it was with the fury of a creator that he imposed laws upon matter. Before he painted the Quinta del Sordo, where this passion showed itself in frenzied struggles, we see it in certain details of *The Madhouse*, in the whiteness of the dress of great ladies, for instance the silks of the Countess of Chinchon (the unfortunate wife of Godoy) and in popular figures like *The Water-Carrier* and *The Knife-Grinder* (Budapest). He was already searching for true expression through colour—colour which was brought to life by the forward thrust of the brush-strokes, rather than by its place in the general harmony.

We find this new use of colour both in San Antón de la Florida and in certain oil paintings.

Thus the great crowds of *Tauromaquia* and the *Disparates* are streaked with the constant back-and-forth movement of his burin. Elsewhere the paint is thick, full of granules as though he had added sand or straw, and as though in moving from one colour to another he had stroked them with the same brush. This gives a sensation of intensity, lightness, opacity, transparency. The observer cannot escape the sensations produced by this exceptional treatment of materials.

Goya was a painter of everything—saints, girls, sick and tortured children, brigands and duchesses, priests, generals and actors, distinguished economists, ogres, witches and angels, black he-goats and hysterical mobs, madmen and sages; he achieved the most subtle grey, the jettiest blacks, the tenderest greens and the bloodiest reds. He passed from heaven to hell, from the palace to the street, to that shadowy zone in which the spirit is rarefied like the air we breathe. Goya, official and proscribed, decorated and exiled, pensioned and wanted by the police, strove to win the slow liberation of colour and light. He began with cartoons for tapestries to adorn the rooms of the children of Their Majesties, then he turned to painting the rough features of a smith, the hooded cloak swathing a two-headed monster in the *Disparates*, and ended with the great riot of paintings for the Quinta del Sordo, done with a more restrained palette, but full of shafts of light which even the brightest works of the Mannerists and the Impressionists have not surpassed.

Goya's complete works amount to 566 paintings (more than 700 according to the authors of analytical catalogues) and about 300 engravings: it is certainly not possible to summarise his work in a few words, or to assert that his new use of colour makes him a precursor of the Impressionists.

That is too abstract a theory, since we find in Goya foretastes of Surrealism, Fauvism and Expressionism. If we took a detail from one of his works and made a photographic enlargement of it, many contemporary artists might think that it was from a modern painting. It is not easy to give a man his place in history; in Goya's case we can compare him to a character from the *Disparates:* Bobalicón. This fairy-tale giant holds castanets in his hands, and can beat out rhythms to which all must dance—fair maidens or madmen, youths like Javier Goya or kings like Charles IV, the witches alighting from their flying broomsticks, and old men, and the beautiful Isabella de Corbos. Bobalicón is of magic birth (he came out of a broken bottle, according to a Saracen fable) and can do anything. He can transform himself into a ribboned *Maja* or an old woman, a prince or a mountain warrior sniping against the French invasion. He can attack a duchess's carriage in a lonely pass, or courtesously sweep off his hat and offer his hand to help her alight, or carry her off to some cave and rape her deliciously. He can be St Anthony or the Pope or a madman who thinks he is the Pope. He needs no mask, but takes what features he will, handsome like the Duke of San Carlos; or he assumes the round pale face of a girl reading a love-letter under a parasol.

If Goya had lived in classical times, the priests would have placed him among the gods, and the people in some intermediate category.

A centaur?

Yes, if we can think of this figure galloping either through earthly meadows or along the celestial shores. The animal part, the human face, his divine genius do not make of him a monster, but rather a being for which the division of species and categories has no meaning, a being who is universally present.

Goya. fecit. año. 1815

Goya's life is mysterious. He is known to have had 20 children, of whom only one survived, but their dates of birth and death are unknown. We must not forget that every year after his marriage, Goya had a hope, a joy and a drama.
We have stressed the political events to the extent to which he was involved in them as a Spaniard, as a man, and as an artist.

1746	Francisco Goya was born on March 30th at Fuendetodos, in the home of his maternal relatives, of country gentleman stock. Goya had three brothers: Tomas, the eldest, became a gilder like his father; Camillo, the youngest, became a priest and through Goya obtained the chaplaincy of Chinchon. He also had two sisters.
1747	Death of Philip V, grandson of Louis XIV, the first Bourbon to reign in Spain in succession to the Hapsburgs. Beginning of the reign of Ferdinand VI.
1754	Treatise on the origins of inequality by J. J. Rousseau.
1755	Renewal of the Anglo-French war.
1758	Goya became a pupil in the workshop of José Luzan, a specialist in religious subjects, after following a course in design. He studied at the school of Father Joaquin, where he became a friend of Martin Zapater.
1759	Beginning of the reign of Charles III.
1761	Charles III summoned Tiepolo to decorate his palace at Madrid. A. R. Mengs arrived at Madrid and took office as Court painter.
1762	Goya's first known work, the paintings for the reliquary of the parish church of Fuendetodos, destroyed in 1936.
1763	Goya fled from Fuendetodos as a result of a brawl, and went to Madrid. He entered the competition for the Academy of San Fernando. The subject for the pencil drawing was the Statue of Silenus. The scholarship was awarded to Gregorio Ferro. F. Bayeu settled at Court.
1764	Dissolution of the Society of Jesus in France. Publication of Voltaire's Dictionary of Philosophy.

1766	Aranda, who supported the ideas of the French Encyclopedists, became Charles III's Chief Minister.
1767	The Jesuits were expelled from Europe and Spanish America.
1770	Tiepolo died at Madrid, where he had completed the decoration of the vault of the throne-room. He was succeeded by Mengs, who in his turn favoured F. Bayeu.
1771	Goya went to Rome. Legend has it that he joined a company of bullfighters. He entered the competition of the Academy of Parma. The theme: Hannibal looks down from the Alps on Italy for the first time. He obtained six votes and an honourable mention. The *Portrait of Manuel Vargas Machuca* is a relic of this visit. After six months Goya returned to Saragossa where he had a client. On October 21st he received his first important commission, the decoration of the choir vault in the Chapel of the Virgin.
1772	In January he presented the sketch which was accepted by the Office of Works without waiting for the approval of the Royal Academy.
1773	Clement XIV dissolved the Company of Jesus. On July 25th Goya married Josefa, Bayeu's sister. First self-portrait, of which only copies exist.
1774	Decoration of the Charterhouse of the Aula Dei at Saragossa. Seven compositions painted in oils between April and November. Goya was summoned by Mengs to Madrid. He settled with Josefa near the Bayeu family in the Calle del Reloj.
1775	Birth of José Ramon, perhaps his first child. Goya made his debut as a painter of tapestry cartoons. He submitted a first series of cartoons in May and a second in October.
1777	Birth of Vicente Anastasio. Goya was seriously ill. Painted and submitted about ten cartoons.
1778	Cartoon of the *Blind Guitarist*, of which he made an etching. Visit of the architect Sabatani to Goya's studio; he took away a few sketches. Goya made some engravings after Velasquez.

1779

Presentation of works to the king. Birth of Maria del Pilar. On Meng's death he asked to be appointed Court painter; his request was refused. Painted 12 cartoons including *The Washerwomen*.

1780

Paper money was put in circulation. Birth of Francisco de Paula. Goya was nominated a member of the Academy of San Fernando. With his candidature he submitted a Christ on the Cross. In May the Office of Works of the Cathedral of the Pillar at Saragossa commissioned Goya to paint one of the cupolas at a fee of 3,000 pesos.

1781

Death of Goya's father, a gilder by trade. Goya finished his work for the cathedral after some quarrels with F. Bayeu who was responsible for the entire decoration.
Commission of the Crown for the basilica of St. Francis.
Subject: St Bernardine of Siena preaching before King Alfonso V of Aragon.

1782

Birth of Ermenegilda. Small *Portrait of Cornelius van der Gotten*, Director of the Royal Tapestry Factory, the only portrait dating from this year.

1783

Beaumarchais' *Marriage of Figaro* was performed in Paris.
Spain had taken part in the American War of Independence and received Minorca and Florida in the Treaty of Versailles. Goya made friends with the King's brother, the Infante Louis of Bourbon. He spent the months of August and September with him, and painted the prince, his morganatic wife and his two children, Luis, future Cardinal of Toledo, and Maria Teresa, future Countess of Chinchon, the wife of Godoy. Returning to Madrid, Goya sent for his mother and his brother Camilo, who was to become chaplain of Chinchon. According to Camilo's confidences to Zapater, Goya was disgusted at the attacks against him, and turned against painting.

1784

With the help of Melchior de Jovellanos he obtained a commission for four large canvases for a college of the University of Salamanca, destroyed during the war against Napoleon.
Birth of Francisco Javier, his only child to survive.
Portrait of the architect Ventura Rodriguez.

1785	Death of the Infante Luis. The Bank of San Carlos commissioned a series of portraits. On May 17th Goya was appointed Assistant Director of Painting at the Academy of San Fernando (annual honorarium 12 doubloons). The new patrons were the Duke and Duchess of Osuna and the Duke and Duchess of Medinaceli. Commission for an Annunciation for San Antón del Prado. *Portrait of the Duchess of Osuna.*
1786	He began to enjoy a certain material security. Interest on his capital, over and above the honorarium from the Academy and his commissions, gave him an income of about 12 thousand reales a year. He was appointed painter to the king at 15,000 reales a year. He bought a luxury carriage, and then had an accident. *Portrait of Bayeu. Portrait of Charles III in Court dress.*
1787	Much work: 7 canvases commissioned by the Osuna family at a price of 22 thousand reales. In France the Edict of Fontainbleau restored religious and civil liberty to Protestants. The United States Constitution was passed. At the census there were more than 10 million Spaniards.
1788	Convocation of the States General in France. *Portrait of the Countess of Altamira and her daughter.* Candidate for the Directorship of Painting at the Academy. Looked for the best way to invest 100 thousand reales. Compiled the inventory of works of art in the royal residences. Death of Charles III.
1789	Charles IV, son of the previous monarch, husband of Maria Luisa of Parma, was proclaimed king on January 14th. He appointed Goya Court painter. Goya took the oath on April 30th at Aranjuez. July 14th, capture of the Bastille. Coronation of Charles IV in September, for which Goya painted some portraits.
1790	Goya sent off the portraits painted by order of Charles IV for his brother the king of Naples. He went to Saragossa for the festival of the Virgin of the Pillar, and painted the *Portrait of Zapater.*
1791	Louis XVI accepted the Constitution.

| 1792 | Fall of Louis XVI. Aranda gave up his office to Godoy, favourite of Maria Luisa. Kellermann's victory at Valmy.
Illness which caused Goya's deafness. |

| 1793 | Goya was deaf.
Execution of Louis XVI.
The Convention declared war on Spain. |

| 1794 | Beginning of the Terror.
Fall of Robespierre. Church and State separated in France.
The French invaded Catalonia. Portrait of the actress *La Tirana*.
Popular Amusements. The Madhouse. The painter Esteve became the official copyist of Goya's portraits. |

| 1795 | Re-opening of the churches in France.
Suppression of the Revolutionary Tribunal. Constitution of the year III. The Directory.
Portrait of the Duke and Duchess of Alba.
Peace of Basle signed with the French.
Death of F. Bayeu.
Sketch of Goya on horseback. The Academy elected Goya Director of Painting in preference to Gregorio Ferro.
Alliance of Spain with the Directory by the Treaty of San Ildefonso. Spain was at war with England.
Death of the Duke of Alba.
Goya stayed with the Duchess.
Series of gouaches foreshadowing the *Caprichos*. |

| 1797 | Bonaparte's victory at Rivoli.
The publication of the *Caprichos* announced.
Portrait of the Duchess of Alba dressed in black.
The Duke and Duchess of Osuna bought six pictures with scenes of witchcraft. |

| 1798 | Bonaparte's victory at the Pyramids.
The English recapture Minorca. *Portrait of the Ambassador* and *Portrait of Jovellanos.*
Frescoes of San Anton de la Florida at Madrid. |

| 1799 | Bonaparte returned to France.
Publication of the *Caprichos;* withdrawn from circulation after 27 copies had been sold.
The Osuna family bought 7 pictures of folk-scenes.
Goya was appointed first painter of the Bedchamber after painting the portraits of the sovereigns. |

1800	Bonaparte's victory at Marengo. *Portrait of the Countess of Chinchon*, wife of Godoy. *Portrait of the family of Charles IV.*
1801	Assassination of Paul I. Alexander I proclaimed Tsar. *Portrait of Godoy in General's uniform* in the war of the House of Orange against Portugal.
1802	Bonaparte became life Consul. Peace of Amiens, end of hostilities with England. Minorca restored into the possession of Spain. Death of the Duchess of Alba. Goya participated in plans for a funeral monument.
1803	Goya made over the *Caprichos* to the King for an annual income of 12 thousand reales for his son Javier. He bought a house in Madrid as an investment for 80 thousand reales.
1804	Coronation of Napoleon I. Goya tried to become Director General of the Academy, but Gregorio Ferro was successful, as he was at the time of the competition in 1763. *Portrait of the Marquis of San Adrian.*
1805	The French entered Vienna. The Franco-Spanish fleet of Admirals Villeneuve and Gravina annihilated by Nelson at Trafalgar. The Historical Academy commissioned from Goya the *Portrait of José de Vargas Ponce*, its Director. Marriage of Javier with Gumersinda Goicoechea. Full-length portraits of the couple. *Portrait of the Marquesa of Santa Cruz*, daughter of the Duke and Duchess of Osuna. Death of Chopinot, antiquarian, restauranteur and collector of Goya. Godoy wished to create a kingdom for himself in part of Portugal. France sent 15 thousand men into Germany and Denmark under the Marquis de la Romana. The party opposing Godoy was led by the future Ferdinand VII. Goya's career as a portraitist was at its peak.
1806	Continental blockade imposed by Napoleon. Dissolution of the German Holy Roman Empire. *Portrait of Isabella Cobos.* Inauguration of the Royal Military Institute, founded by Godoy; Goya painted its coat of arms. Portrait of Godoy, canvas destroyed in 1808.

1807	Ferdinand gathered together a band of conspirators and organised a plot. His father had him arrested. The trial at the Escorial ended with a pardon.
1808	Revolt of Aranjuez. Charge against Godoy. Ferdinand VII entered Madrid. Charles IV had abdicated in his favour. Confiscation of Godoy's possessions including the two Majas by Goya. The Academy of San Fernando commissioned Goya to paint the portrait of the new king. Ferdinand posed on April 6th and 7th. Beginning of the War of Independence. Capitulation of Bailen. Joseph Bonaparte nominated King of Spain. Napoleon arranged for the old sovereign and the new, Maria Luisa and Godoy to meet at Biarritz and offered Ferdinand the crown of Etruria, but he refused. On May 2nd the Royal Princes refused to obey Murat's order to go to Bayonne, and the people revolted. Attack on the Mamelukes at the Porta del Sol. Executions by shooting. Abdication of Ferdinand VII. Goya went to Saragossa to paint the city's defence against the French troops. The assembly of representatives of the country and the colonies adopted a Constitution of the Napoleonic type with Joseph Bonaparte as King. Meeting of Napoleon and Alexander I at Erfurt. Victory of Somosierra which made it possible to re-take Madrid, which Joseph abandoned after Bailen. Goya was in the group of 30 thousand families who swore loyalty to him on December 23rd.
1809	Napoleon conquered Vienna. Revolt of the Tyrol against France. Excommunication of Napoleon. The English landed in Portugal. One single dated portrait: *The Marquesa of Santiago*.
1810	Napoleon married Marie Louise of Austria. He annexed the Netherlands and the German coast on the North Sea. Soult conquered almost the whole of Andalusia. Sympathy for the liberal reforms led to the rise of the *afrancesados* (of whom Goya was one). Goya completed a large allegorical composition painted in honour of Joseph at the request of the municipality of Madrid. This allegory was altered to glorify the heroes of May 2nd. Goya was given the task of choosing 50 pictures to be sent to the Musée Napoléon in Paris. He drew up a will with his wife. He etched some scenes: *The Disasters of War*.

1811	Birth of the King of Rome.
1812	Capture and burning of Moscow. Souchet occupied Valencia. Wellington defeated Marmount at Arapiles. The Constitution proclaiming national sovereignty and unity approved by Ferdinand VII. Death of Josefa; Javier claimed his mother's inheritance. The inventory of his pictures shows that Goya possessed 4 prints by Wouvermans, 10 prints by Rembrandt, 2 landscapes by Perelle, a collection of Piranasi's work, a head by Correggio, 2 pictures by Tiepolo, a self-portrait by Velasquez. Goya painted a series of portraits of Wellington.
1813	Defeat of the French at Leipzig. Wellington beat the French at Victoria and freed Bidassoa. Napoleon restored the throne to Ferdinand VII, who, by the Treaty of Valencay, promised to expel the English and respect the *afrancesados*. There are no works by Goya dated 1813.
1814	Fall of Napoleon. First restoration in France. Reception of Ferdinand VII at the Academy. Goya painted many portraits of the monarch, *The second of May*, and *The shootings of the 3rd May*.
1815	Napoleon returned from the island of Elba. Waterloo. Goya painted a great deal.
1816	*Portrait of the Duke of Osuna and his sister*. Goya completed the *Tauromachia* series and the *Disasters of War*.
1817	Last work carried out for the Royal Palace at Madrid.
1818	No dated pictures.
1819	Goya bought the Quinta del Sordo outside Madrid for 60 thousand reales. Commissioned to paint the large picture *The last Communion of St Joseph of Colasan*. Fell ill. Worked on the last series of engravings, the *Disparates*. The Academy was to publish these in 1864. Death of Charles IV at Naples and Maria Luisa at Rome.

1820	Coup d'état of General Riego who restored constitutional monarchy. Painting dedicated to Doctor Arrietta. Goya present at the swearing of the oath of loyalty to the new Constitution. Cohabited with Leocadia Zorilla, a distant relative.
1821	Liberation of Greece. Death of Napoleon on St. Helena. "Black" paintings for the Quinta del Sordo.
1822	Ferdinand VII sought French aid, and the army under the leadership of the Duke of Angoulême restored absolute monarchy. General Riego killed. Goya gave his possessions to his grandson Mariano.
1823	Death of Louis XVIII. Charles X King of France. Goya obtained permission to go to Plombières for a thermal cure. Settled in Bordeaux.
1825	Death of Alexander I, Tsar of Russia. Nomination of Nicholas I. Goya asked for his permission to be renewed. Made some lithographs with his friend the printer Goulon. Went to Paris where, it is said, he met Gros, Gericault and Delacroix.
1826	Returned to Madrid, asked to retire and obtained a pension and permission to return to France. Vincente Lopez painted the *Portrait of Goya* which is now in the Prado.
1827	Probable second visit to Madrid. Painted *The Milkmaid of Bordeaux* and *Jose Pio de Molina*, his two last works.
1828	Lost the power of speech and remained semi-paralysed. Died in the night of the 15th April. Buried first at Bordeaux, then at Madrid, at San Antón de la Florida.

Chronological table compiled by Catherine Valogne.

BIBLIOGRAPHY

This is a list of books considered essential for a complete study of the artist's work.

J. Adhemar   *Goya*
                    Paris - 1941

A. Beruete y Moret *Goya as a portrait painter*
                    London - 1922

Desparmet Fitzgerald *L'oeuvre peint de Goya*
                    Paris - 1928/50

G. Estrada   *Bibliografia de Goya*
                    Mexico - 1940

P. Gassier   *Goya*
                    Cleveland - 1955

José Gudiol   *Goya*
                    Barcelone - 1970

A. L. Huxeley   *The complete etchings of Goya*
                    New York - 1943

A. Malraux   *Dessins de Goya*
                    Paris - 1947

A. Mayer   *F. de Goya*
                    London - 1924

H. Rothe   *F. Goya*
                    Munich - 1943

A. Ruiz Cabriada   *Aportacion à una bibliografia de Goya*
                    Madrid - 1946

F. J. Sanchez Canton *Goya*
                    New York - 1964